New Ways of
Looking at Old Texts, II

Papers of the Renaissance
English Text Society, 1992–1996

MEDIEVAL & RENAISSANCE
TEXTS & STUDIES

VOLUME 188

RENAISSANCE ENGLISH TEXT SOCIETY
SPECIAL PUBLICATION

Josephine A. Roberts
November 11, 1948–August 26, 1996

New Ways of
Looking at Old Texts, II

Papers of the Renaissance
English Text Society, 1992–1996

edited by

W. SPEED HILL

Medieval & Renaissance Texts & Studies
in conjunction with
Renaissance English Text Society
Tempe, Arizona
1998

Library of Congress Cataloging-in-Publication Data

New ways of looking at old texts. II : papers of the Renaissance English Text
  Society, 1992–1996 / edited by W. Speed Hill.
      p. cm. — (Medieval & Renaissance texts & studies ; v. 188) (Renaissance
  English Text Society special publication)
      Includes index.
      ISBN 0-86698-230-2
      1. English literature—Early modern, 1500–1700—Criticism, Textual.
  2. Manuscripts, Renaissance—England—Editing.   3. Manuscripts, English—
  Editing. 4. Paleography, English. 5. Renaissance—England. I. Hill, W. Speed
  (William Speed), 1935– .   II. Renaissance English Text Society.   III. Series.
  IV. Series: Renaissance English Text Society special publication.
  PR418.T48N49 1998
  820.9 '003—dc21   98–19258
                                                                                       CIP

This book is made to last.
It is set in Bembo, smythe-sewn,
and printed on acid-free paper
to library specifications.

Printed in the United States of America

To the memory of

JOSEPHINE A. ROBERTS

Contents

Preface

Like its predecessor volume, *New Ways of Looking at Old Texts [I]: Papers of the Renaissance English Text Society, 1985–1991*, the present volume, *New Ways . . . II* (alternate titles considered were: *Newer Ways . . .* and *New Ways . . . The Sequel*), prints papers given at the national MLA conventions from 1992 through 1996. It is a slimmer volume, as it covers five, not six, years, and it includes no occasional lectures. Nonetheless, the claim made on behalf of the earlier volume ("read chronologically [the essays] supply a useful proxy for developments in the field . . .") remains valid for this collection as well. Although thirteen of the fifteen contributors write as practicing editors and all address editorial issues—or, in one case (Gants), bibliographical issues—the topical range is extensive. Recurrent editorial topoi—choice of copy-text (Pigman, Solopova, Levenson), choice of editorial models (Hill, King, Urkowitz, Lavagnino), historical philology and "old spelling" (Richardson), annotation (Faulkner, King), the role of external fact (Faulkner, Werstine)—reappear, and newer ones—the impact of poststructuralism (Levenson, Urkowitz), canon formation (Taylor, Briggs, Paster), the structure of electronic texts (Lavagnino, Urkowitz), the use of computer-based analysis to construct a stemma (Solopova)—make their debuts.

A obvious limitation of such a collection, especially when nearly all its contributors are working editors, is the all but irresistible inclination to construct essays on a this-is-what-I-did-and-this-is-why-I-did-it model, as if editing were merely a matter of procedure and methodology, uninfluenced by ideology, detached from wider literary and/or scholarly issues, comfortably empiricist in its ontology and positivist in its epistemology. Pigman, Levenson, Solopova, and myself fall into that category, but two of us—Pigman and myself—are responding to the topic set for the session, *"Problems in the Selection of Copy-Text,"* that invited such a rhetoric of response. (At least in my case, the topic is inverted: "what-I-*didn't*-do-and-why-I-*didn't*-do-it.") Nonetheless, what is noteworthy about this collection is the range of topics treated that, while prompted by editorial activity, are not usually thought of as "editorial" issues.

On the one hand, Elizabeth Solopova (together with her colleague Peter Robinson) tackles an orthodox problem: what surviving document of the *Canterbury Tales* should be the basis for establishing a critical text? The problem is defined traditionally as discovering "what Chaucer is likely to have written." The novelty resides in combined power of two computer-based tools of analysis: Robinson's program *Collate*, and what evolutionary biologists call cladistic analysis ("the systematic classification of groups of organisms on the basis of the order of their assumed divergence from ancestral species," my *New Shorter Oxford English Dictionary* explains). She concludes that the Hengwrt, not the Ellesmere, is closer to Chaucer and so should be the basis for a critical text of his *Tales*. Her aim is not new at all: it is to reconstruct a missing archetype through recensionist analysis of the text in the surviving documents. What is new is the technology brought to bear on the problem. Issues of procedure and methodology are central because of the wealth of that surviving documentation. Using hand-eye collation, John Manly and Edith Rickert were famously unable to construct a viable stemma for the *Canterbury Tales* after spending two scholarly lifetimes trying. Solopova's and Robinson's claim that they have—or at least are demonstrably on their way to doing so—will doubtless be scrutinized by other working editors of Chaucer, but their claim of success is nonetheless arresting—and disturbing, for it means "that the tens of thousands of students who every year read the *Canterbury Tales* in the *Riverside Chaucer,* based on Ellesmere, are reading a text at many points far removed from what Chaucer is likely to have written" (128).

On the other hand, the entire panel for 1995, "*Editing as Canon Construction: The Case of Middleton,*" assesses the impact on the canon of Renaissance drama of the forthcoming Oxford edition of Middleton's complete works. Provocatively suggesting that, *pace* Shakespeare, you can no longer have it both ways, its general editor, Gary Taylor, asserts that Middleton's moral realism has been unfairly overshadowed by his older canonical contemporary. Still, one of the Middleton editors, Gail Kern Paster, reads the promotion of Middleton to the status of a romantic "author" of a "collected works" against the grain of Taylor's campaign to secure for Middleton a higher perch on the canonical ladder by showing why the plays written for the boys of St. Paul's ought not to be lumped with plays written for the adult players of the King's Men. Her essay, "The Children's Middleton," emerges from her careful reconstruction of a very local context—St. Paul's Cathedral and its immediate precincts—as sub-genre within a collected works that inevitably incorporates every item as a "work" of one "author." Yet another Middleton editor, Julia

Briggs, is quite happy to welcome *The Second Maiden's Tragedy* (or *The Lady's /
Ladies' Tragedy*) back into the canon of Middleton's authentic works, not only
for the interest of the play itself for contemporary academic audiences, but
because by subsuming it under the category of "author" and by revising the
chronology of his "works," its text may be read afresh, and a developmental
arc constructed for an authorial oeuvre based on that new chronology. Canon
formation is not usually thought of as an editorial issue, but as Taylor inven-
tively reiterates, it is in fact the foundation of editing: which author do you
edit? which plays/texts do you include, and which do you exclude? which attributions do you accept or reject? which multiple-text plays do you accord
multiple-version status within an edition? which parts of jointly authored texts
do you print, and under whose name? All these are questions editors routinely
face, though rarely are they articulated so clearly.

Nothing would seem more removed from the tedious chores of collation,
computer-assisted or manual, that are the foundation of the editor's activities
than the heady speculations of poststructuralism. Yet for over two millennia
editors have lived with issues of fragmentalism, multiple versions, authorial as
well as textual indeterminacy, and intertextuality. From the vantage point of
the textual critic, it is the poststructuralists who are late to the feast. Still, it is
one thing to argue that *Romeo and Juliet* is an indeterminately multiple text (as
Jonathan Goldberg has); it is something quite different to accommodate that
textual multiplicity to the demands of a commercial publisher's series specifications. Just how the two—poststructuralist speculation and textual specificity—
intersect is the burden of Jill Levenson's account of what *she* did editing the
Oxford *Romeo and Juliet*. The same pairing, poststructuralist analysis and textual specificity, form the warp and woof of Paul Werstine's meditation on the
Shakespeare's historical anachronisms. He takes editors to task for correcting
history in *Richard III* as if the Bard were a beginning undergraduate major in
history who somehow couldn't get his facts straight and needed a professorial
vetting to sort out names, titles, and chronology. The issue is a perennial one,
codified by G. Thomas Tanselle (*SB* 29) in "External Fact as an Editorial
Problem"; Werstine treats it with a deft sophistication. That the multiplicities
poststructuralism authorizes can in turn authorize a variety of theatrical interpretations is Steve Urkowitz's theme, as he teases a pair of textual variants in
King Lear into multiple interpretive possibilities. In oral delivery as a conference paper, Urkowitz's varying intonations of the line variously given
Gloucester (Quarto) and "Cor." (Folio [Cornwall? Cordelia?]), "Heere's
France and Burgundy, my Noble Lord," dispute Derrida's preference for writing over speech, for there is no way to notate in the impoverished medium
of print the nuanced differences between each of the four ways a textually
identical sentence was actually delivered. Though not a working editor—

indeed, he has positioned himself as of the school of "unediting"—Urkowitz suggests that the riches of the CD-ROM medium ought to release from a work a multiplicity of textual options heretofore imprisoned in the limitations of the printed codex format of a single text subscribed with cryptic textual notes below.

In reviews of the earlier *New Ways* volume, Tim William Machan (*TEXT* 9) and David Greetham (*MP* 93) each remarked on the underlying consensus of its contributors that the issues occupying contemporary editors were now being refracted through the socialized editing model of Jerome McGann and not the intentionalist one of Greg, Bowers, and Tanselle. That consensus is not evident in this volume. All three editors in the 1992 session work within the older paradigm, adjusting it to the requirements of the author being edited. G. W. Pigman bases his Oxford edition of Gascoigne's poems on his *A Hundreth Sundrie Flowres* even though it admittedly does not represent Gascoigne's "final intentions," as *The Posies* does. The Faulkner–Kiessling–Blair text of Burton's *Anatomy of Melancholy* is based on the fourth edition (1632), as it is the one most comprehensively realizing the evolving intentions of Burton's life work. That copy-text is emended from the 1638 and 1651 editions (the last posthumous), where Burton has added material or revised his text. Nothing could be more orthodox. Faulkner's paper supplies examples of Burton's own on-going engagement with the religious/political issues of the day, notably the sabbatarian controversy, as revealed in the revisions that textual collation has filtered out from the huge textual corpus. Janel Mueller's edition of the writings of Queen Katherine Parr focuses more narrowly on the work of an individual author. To do so she situates Parr circumstantially in her own very local social world as the sixth wife of Henry VIII. As I observed in the introduction to *New Ways [I]* (23), editors of women's writings in the early modern period resist having their newly recovered authors subsumed within a leveling socialization of authorship, and the recovery of individual authorial intention remains foundational for their editions.

On another scale entirely, how can one individuate authorial intention from socialized welter of John Foxe's martyrology, the "Book of Martyr's"—a "book" that is less codex than archive? John N. King's survey of the problems of editing such a work is sobering, and one can only hope that those now at work on it in England have some theoretical as well as methodological grasp of the issues involved. To be sure, procedure and methodology will always be a refuge when the data threaten to overwhelm the editor, as is surely the case with Foxe's juggernaut, but editing is more than accuracy of transcription and fidelity to the document at hand. Even with the reproductive powers of the CD-ROM and the disseminatory potential of the Internet, an archive does not an edition make, as John Lavagnino acutely observes. For the edited work to be truly accessible (as the technology keeps promising it will), it needs an editorial infrastructure of introductions, commentary, glosses, chronology, line-numbers, etc., if the reader/user is to be well served. An editorial proto-col suited to displaying the well-wrought urn behind modernist glass—as the Greg–Bowers–Tanselle model was superbly designed to do, is unlikely to serve so well when the artifact is Foxe's gargantuan archive.

Although the profession seems bent on ghettoizing editing as it has bibli-ography, the evidence of the papers in this collection suggests that there is in practice more permeability between the world of the interpreter and the world of the editor than is generally acknowledged. Textual critics turn out to be astute hermeneuts, and critics are beginning to realize the interpretive utili-ty of the materials that editorial inquiry turns up. Indeed, most editors do not start out professionally to be or become editors. Rather, they encounter mat-erial in the course of their research that begs to be edited—the heretofore largely invisible writings of early modern women are a salient example, as is Foxe's all too visible "Book of Martyr's." Such scholars become editors in mid-career, driven by their interest of works heretofore inaccessible. Such edi-tors do not stop interpreting when they start editing. To be sure, they may be curtailed in their speculations by the irreducible facticity of the textual data (or absence of textual data) and the stubbornly material limitations of the surviv-ing documents (although the paucity of surviving evidence has not noticeably inhibited Shakespearean editors). But, by the same token, their editorially de-rived speculations have—potentially, at least—an evidential basis that is firmer and more carefully drawn than that found in many contemporary new histori-cist meditations unanchored in the textual history of the texts under review.

This, I would argue, is the intellectual rationale for the present collection. The papers included in this volume do not merely list or cite items of textual data; rather, they use these data as the foundation for searching discussions of interpretive issues that necessarily must be revisited, again and again: not merely "what the author wrote," but which author? when did he or she write it? what did he or she intend to mean? who was the audience then? since? now? what was the reception? and how are all these issues to be incorporated in the editions we produce and read? These quite traditional issues are all the more pertinent to a world where poststructuralist critiques have questioned many traditional editorial procedures and goals.

§

The frontispiece and dedication of this volume are wholly inadequate tes-timony to the debt all scholars and editors of Renaissance texts owe Jo Roberts whose tragic death on August 26, 1996, left us all shaken. As the editor of *The Poems of Lady Mary Wroth* (1983) and *The First Part of The Countess of Montgomery's Urania* (1995), she was at work on the latter's manuscript continuation at the time of her death. That important work is being continued by the Society (principally by Janel Mueller and Suzanne Gossett) in respectful tribute to our memory of her as a person and to her professional contributions to the field.

W. SPEED HILL

Editing Revised Texts:
Gascoigne's A Hundredth Sundrie Flowres *and* The Posies

G. W. PIGMAN III

O VER THE PAST FIFTEEN YEARS THE CONTROVERSY CONCERN-
ing Shakespearean revision has increased awareness about some of
the problems involved in editing revised texts. Those who believe
that the Folio *King Lear* is Shakespeare's own revision of an earlier version of
the play, represented by the first Quarto, insist that editors should not conflate
the two versions, as has been customary since the eighteenth century.[1] As a
general principle I would agree that one should not conflate distinct versions
of a text, but determining in individual cases just what constitutes conflation
is often no easy task. Moreover, Shakespeare's stature obscures a practical
problem facing editors of less important authors. Since the market can bear
separate editions of the Quarto and Folio *Lear*, one need not choose between
them. An editor of George Gascoigne does not have the luxury of printing
both the first and second editions.[2] But even if one did, one might choose

---

[1] Stanley Wells, "Introduction: The Once and Future *King Lear*," in *The Division
of the Kingdoms: Shakespeare's Two Versions of* King Lear, ed. Gary Taylor and Michael
Warren (1983; rpt. Oxford: Oxford Univ. Press, 1986), 1–22, and Grace Ioppolo,
Revising Shakespeare (Cambridge: Harvard Univ. Press, 1991), 19–43.

[2] When electronic editions become more sophisticated and more accepted, this
practical difficulty will disappear, but at present they pose their own problems, not the
least of which is expense. For an acute discussion of electronic editions, see John

not to. For it is difficult to decide whether *A Hundreth Sundrie Flowres* and *The Posies* are two different works or two editions of the same work. I shall argue that they should be regarded as different works, even though the text of most of the pieces from the first edition remains substantially the same in the second. Regarding the two editions as separate works then raises the problem of conflation, since Gascoigne's revisions fall into two classes that can be easily distinguished sometimes but not at others: revisions designed to make an individual work conform to a new conception of the work as a whole and revisions designed to improve the individual work as an individual work. I try to accept into my text only those variants from the second edition that appear to be Gascoigne's revisions and that appear only to affect the individual work as an individual work. By choosing not to use the revised edition as copy-text, I have had to confront another problem that bedevils the editor of revised texts, and I shall try to justify my decision not to use the edition that definitely represents Gascoigne's final intention.[3]

In 1573 and 1575 Gascoigne published two collections of his work that differ in three major ways. First, the 1573 edition is presented as an anthology on the order of Tottel's *Songes and Sonettes*. No author or editor is mentioned on the title page, which reads: *A Hundreth sundrie Flowres bounde up in one small Poesie. Gathered partely (by translation) in the fyne outlandish Gardins of Euripides, Ovid, Petrarke, Ariosto, and others: and partly by invention, out of our owne fruitefull Orchardes in Englande: Yelding sundrie sweete savours of Tragical, Comical, and Morall Discourses, bothe pleasaunt and profitable to the well smellyng noses of learned Readers.*[4] Curiously placed prefatory letters explain that one H. W. is responsible for printing this collection of "divers discourses and

---

Lavagnino, "Reading, Scholarship, and Hypertext Editions," *TEXT* 8 (1995): 109–124.

[3] My edition is scheduled to appear in the Oxford English Texts of Oxford University Press. The first two editors of Gascoigne use *The Posies* as their copy-text; the next two use *A Hundreth Sundrie Flowres*, although neither one includes the plays: *The Complete Poems of George Gascoigne*, ed. William Carew Hazlitt (London: Whittingham & Wilkins, 1869–70); *The Complete Works of George Gascoigne*, ed. John W. Cunliffe (Cambridge: Cambridge Univ. Press, 1907–10); *A Hundreth Sundrie Flowres From the Original Edition*, ed. B. M. Ward (London: Etchells and MacDonald, 1926; 2nd edition with additions by Ruth Lloyd Miller, Jennings, LA: Minos Publishing, 1975); *George Gascoigne's* A Hundreth Sundrie Flowres, ed. C. T. Prouty (Columbia, MO: Univ. of Missouri, 1942). All citations from Gascoigne are from my edition, but I give page references to the first volume of Cunliffe's.

[4] Both editions acknowledge that Francis Kinwelmarsh translated parts of *Jocasta* and that Christopher Yelverton wrote its epilogue, but the plays are not presented as part of the anthology introduced by H. W.'s and G. T.'s letters, and no author in the anthology, except for Gascoigne himself, is named.

verses, invented uppon sundrie occasions, by sundrie gentlemen" (490).[5] The title page of *The Posies of George Gascoigne Esquire* immediately drops the pretense of multiple authorship, and in three prefatory letters Gascoigne justifies the republication of his work. Second, *The Posies* is almost a quarter longer than *A Hundreth Sundrie Flowres*.[6] Third, although Gascoigne changed the order of the works and most of their titles, he hardly revised any of the texts, except to correct a few errors and, occasionally, to improve a phrase. Hence the texts of the two plays, *Supposes* and *Jocasta*, and of eighty-six poems are substantially the same. Only *The Adventures of Master F. J.* is thoroughly revised; it becomes *The pleasant Fable of Ferdinando Jeronomi and Leonora de Valasco, translated out of the Italian riding tales of Bartello*—a fable with a heavily moralistic beginning and ending. Outside of *Master F. J.* only two poems differ significantly because of revisions. Antipapist sentiments are removed from "A gloze upon this text, *Dominus iis opus habet*" and from "Councell given to master Bartholmew Withipoll."

It is easy to see that *The Posies* is an enlarged edition of *A Hundreth Sundrie Flowres* and that *Master F. J.* has been extensively revised, but that still leaves the bulk of the first edition more or less unchanged. One might say that those minor changes make no difference to the individual works, especially when they are read in isolation, as is usually the case. But the context places many of the poems in a new light because the organization of the two editions differs dramatically. *A Hundreth Sundrie Flowres* is an anthology by diverse gentlemen without patent moral intent, while *The Posies* is a record of Gascoigne's misspent youth, a warning to others that marks the reformation of this prodigal son.

I do not mean to imply that Gascoigne never moralizes in the first edition; the whole question of Gascoigne's reformation is more complicated than

---

[5] It should be noted in passing that there are a number of hints that the collection might be Gascoigne's work and not an anthology, especially the headnote to the first poem in the avowedly Gascoigne section of "The devises of sundrie Gentlemen": "I will now deliver unto you *so many more* of Master Gascoignes Poems as have come to my hands, who hath never beene dayntie of his doings, and therfore I conceale not his name" (478; my emphasis).

[6] *The Posies* adds three prefatory letters, a number of commendatory verses with Gascoigne's response to them, four poems (including "Dulce Bellum inexpertis," which is almost 1,900 lines long), the conclusion of "Dan Bartholmew of Bathe" (marked incomplete in *A Hundreth Sundrie Flowres*), and "Certayne notes of Instruction concerning the making of verse or ryme in English." It omits five poems as well as the original prefatory matter.

Prouty and others have thought.[7] The first edition's "The Printer to the Reader"—a letter Gascoigne wrote himself—contains a concise statement of a traditional defense that will dominate the prefatory letters to the second edition: "... the discrete reader may take a happie example by the most lascivious histories, although the captious and harebrained heads can neither be encoraged by the good, nor forewarned by the bad" (476).[8] But in 1573 this defense is more or less an aside, certainly not the organizing principle it will become two years later in the prefatory letters to *The Posies*: "bicause I have (to mine owne great detriment) mispent my golden time, I may serve as ensample to the youthfull Gentlemen of England, that they runne not upon the rocks which have brought me to shipwracke" (14; cf. 12–14, 16–17). The division of *The Posies* into flowers (more pleasant than profitable), herbs (moral discourses more profitable than pleasant), and weeds (medicinal if rightly handled as warnings) is the structure Gascoigne creates to try to guide the reader toward the right use of his exemplary writings (13). This emphasis on the exemplary nature of Gascoigne's youthful follies coexists somewhat uneasily with a disavowal of the personal, for in 1575 he also contends that he wrote the greater part of the love poetry for other men (16). In any event, the desire to transform the personal into the exemplary motivates a number of

---

[7] C. T. Prouty, *George Gascoigne: Elizabethan Courtier, Soldier, and Poet* (New York: Columbia Univ. Press, 1942), 78–100. Cf. Richard C. McCoy, "Gascoigne's 'Poëmata castrata': The Wages of Courtly Success," *Criticism* 27 (1985): 29–55.

[8] Prouty assumes that the printer wrote "The Printer to the Reader," but the evidence for Gascoigne's authorship is overwhelming. First and foremost, if Henry Bynneman had written a letter to be included in the preliminaries (a letter that was printed after the rest of the book had gone through the press), he would have known that "H. W. to the Reader" does not appear "in the beginning of this worke" (476) but rather after the two plays, more than 100 pages into the work. It is much more likely that Gascoigne wrote the letter, unaware that the plays would come first. Second, the letter elaborates the extended metaphor of the book as a collection of flowers, Gascoigne's "invention" in both the first and second editions. Third, the letter is just the kind of mystification that Gascoigne would enjoy and that makes his work so charming. He creates a fictive printer to cast suspicion upon one fiction—unwilling publication—while continuing another—G. T.'s collection of the devises of sundry gentlemen. Finally, "H. W. to the Reader" contains a strong hint that the printer is fictitious. H. W. refers to him as "my friend *A. B.*" (490); the initials "A. B." are often used to mean "John Doe" (Fredson Thayer Bowers, "Notes on Gascoigne's *A Hundreth Sundrie Flowres* and *The Posies*," *Harvard Studies and Notes in Philology and Literature* 16 [1934]: 13–14; *England's Helicon 1600, 1624*, ed. Hyder Edward Rollins [Cambridge: Harvard Univ. Press, 1935], 2: 67; Franklin B. Williams, Jr., "An Initiation Into Initials," *Studies in Bibliography* 9 [1957]: 165).

small revisions,[9] and one group of barely revised poems shows why one should regard the two collections as distinct works even when the texts are almost identical.

In *A Hundreth Sundrie Flowres* all of the poems presented as Gascoigne's have his name in the title. Since the collection is supposed to be an anthology, the reason for this inclusion is clear. In *The Posies*, however, the author of the entire book has been identified, so one wonders why he retains his name in some titles but removes it from others. Most of the titles from which he removes his name belong to a group of poems at the beginning of the collection, and a plausible explanation can be given for them. *The Posies* opens with the prefatory letters, the commendatory poems, and finally two poems by Gascoigne himself. In the first he defensively offers further justification for the "weeds" in the collection; in the second, "*His ultimum vale* to Amorous verse," he vows to publish no more love poetry. A reader who has made it this far has hardly been favorably disposed to lovers or love poetry. A table of contents for the first division, "Flowers," immediately follows; the first nine items all contain the phrase, "of a lover," beginning with "The Anatomie of a Lover" and ending with "The recantacion of a lover." Not one of the titles in the first edition contains the phrase.

The texts of this group (37–52) have nineteen substantive variants, most of which are on the order of "this" for "his" and are correcting errors that crept into the first edition or are introducing new errors into the second. Only three variants look like revisions, and two of these reinforce the revisions to the titles: Gascoigne removes his last name from the last lines of "The Passion of a Lover" and "The Lullabie of a Lover." He does not try to eliminate the personal completely; he allows his first name to stand in "The arraigment of a Lover" and "The recantacion of a lover." Nevertheless, the pattern is clear. The particularity of Gascoigne's experience gives way to the exemplary experience of "a lover." What is now the first poem of "Flowers" begins: "To make a lover knowne, by playne Anatomie, / You lovers all that list beware, lo here behold you me" (37). That exemplarity was present in the first edition, but the prefatory insistence that "I might yet serve as a myrrour for unbrydled youth, to avoyde those perilles which I had passed" (5) makes it more difficult to hear the playful humor of "Gascoigns Anatomie. The

---

[9] Cf. John Stephens, "George Gascoigne's *Posies* and the Persona in Sixteenth Century Poetry," *Neophilologus* 70 (1986): 130, and G. K. Hunter, "Drab and Golden Lyrics of the Renaissance," in *Forms of Lyric*, ed. Reuben A. Brower (New York: Columbia Univ. Press, 1970), 12.

movement from folly to renunciation now dominates what has become a sequence, and the overall effect resembles what happens to the much more extensively revised *Master F. J.* In the words of George Whetstone's defense of Gascoigne: "And sure these toyes, do showe for your behoof: / The woes of loove, and not the wayes to love."[10]

If you suspect that I prefer the unrevised, less moralized version of Gascoigne's work and that my preference influences my decision to use the first edition as copy-text, you are right. But there is also reason to suspect that, regardless of the sincerity of Gascoigne's presentation of himself as a repentant prodigal from 1575 until the end of his life four years later, he was annoyed at having to yield to external pressure to defend and revise his work. The prefatory letters make it abundantly clear that the major motivation for the revisions in *The Posies* was, in fact, external—an only too justified fear of censorship. On 13 August 1576, "by appointment of the Q. M. Commissioners," Richard Smith, the publisher of *A Hundreth Sundrie Flowres* and *The Posies*, returned "half a hundred of Gascoignes poesies" to the Stationers' Hall.[11] But in any event, there can be no doubt that concern over the reception of the first edition and fear for the second influenced the revisions. The evidence for Gascoigne's annoyance at having to revise comes from some revisions that call the whole project of revision into question.

In his letter "To the reverende Divines" Gascoigne declares: "I understande that sundrie well disposed mindes have taken offence at certaine wanton wordes and sentences passed in the fable of *Ferdinando Jeronimi*, and the Ladie *Elinora de Valasco*" (7). He goes on to assure them that *Master F. J.* has been "gelded from all filthie phrases," to use his words earlier in the letter (6). Given this assurance of *Poëmata castrata*, the sexual pun in the revised title is

---

[10] *A Rembraunce of the wel imployed life, and godly end, of George Gaskoigne Esquire, who deceased at Stalmford in Lincolne Shire the 7. of October. 1577* (London: E. Aggas, 1577), lines 77–78.

[11] *Records of the Court of the Stationers' Company 1576 to 1602 from Register B*, ed. W. W. Greg and E. Boswell (London: The Bibliographical Society, 1930), 86–87. Two other books were returned at the same time, but both were redelivered to their publishers. As Greg remarks (lvii–lviii), the reasons for the confiscation of Gascoigne's work are obscure. Prouty, *George Gascoigne*, 79, thinks that *A Hundreth Sundrie Flowres* was also banned by the Commissioners, but this remains a speculation as records for the period are missing.

startling: "the Italian riding tales."[12] Apparently Gascoigne is mocking the reverend divines with ungelded, but plausibly deniable, puns.

In the letter to the divines Gascoigne also defends himself against the charge that *Master F. J.* was "written to the scandalizing of some worthie personages" (7). Since *The pleasant Fable of Ferdinando Jeronomi and Leonora de Valasco, translated out of the Italian riding tales of Bartello* presents itself as a translation, Gascoigne could easily have rebutted the charge of representing English contemporaries, but he does not even mention Bartello in the prefatory letters. This reticence suggests that one should not take Bartello seriously, and the conclusion to "Dan Bartholmew of Bathe," which is marked as incomplete in the first edition, gives the game away:

> *Bartello* he which writeth ryding tales,
> Bringes in a Knight which cladde was all in greene,
> That sighed sore amidde his greevous gales,
> And was in hold as *Bartholmew* hath beene.
> But (for a placke) it maye therein be seene,
> That, that same Knight which there his griefes begonne,
> Is *Batts* owne Fathers Sisters brothers Sonne. (136)

This stanza is dizzying, a good example of Gascoigne's love of mystifying demystification. As Gascoigne tells us in "Dulce Bellum inexpertis," he was known in the Netherlands by the nickname "the Green Knight" (166). "Bartello" sounds like Bartholomew, and one passage even reads "Battello," an Italianization of "Batt" (375). Three personae—Bartello, the Green Knight, Dan Bartholomew—are collapsing into one person, George Gascoigne. It would take an awfully naive reader not to see Bartello as a fiction.[13]

Gascoigne also casts doubt upon the transposition of the revised *Master F. J.* from England to Italy. As soon as he sets the scene in Italy, he returns to England, "And bicause I do suppose that *Leonora* is the same name whiche wee call *Elinor* in English, and that *Francischina* also doth import none other than *Fraunces*, I will so entitle them as to our own countriemen may be moste

---

[12] The *OED* defines "ride" as "to mount the female; to copulate" (3; cf. 16) and "tail" as "sexual member; penis or (oftener) pudendum" (5c). Helge Kökeritz, *Shakespeare's Pronunciation* (New Haven: Yale Univ. Press, 1953), 149, observes that "tale"/ "tail" is "one of Shakespeare's favorite bawdy puns." In "The lover being disdaynfully abjected by a dame of high calling," Gascoigne, probably recalling Wyatt's "Ye old mule," hurls the insult: "He rydes not me, thou knowest his sadell best" (458).

[13] One not need, however, take the next step and conclude with Prouty, *George Gascoigne*, 218–229, that the stanza shows that "Dan Bartholmew" and *Master F. J.* are autobiographical.

perspicuous" (384).[14] A few lines later Gascoigne casts further suspicion on the Italian setting. *Master F. J.* takes place in the north of England, and F. J. uses a standard Petrarchan conceit in his first letter to Elinor: "... consideringe the naturall clymate of the countrie, I muste say that I have found fire in frost" (384). In the second edition Ferdinando is a Venetian who visits the Lord of Valasco's castle near Florence, which is presumably not much colder than Venice. One might not notice anything strange, if it were not for the marginal note added to the second edition: "The ayre of that Countrie did (by all likelyhood) seeme colder to him than the streetes of Venice." Given that Gascoigne could have picked any Italian cities he liked—F. J. might have come from Naples, for example, a hotter city that Lyly would use as the scene of licentiousness a couple of years later—the decision to make the south colder than the north certainly looks like a joke hinting that a translation from the Italian is a fiction.

But regardless of whether Gascoigne resented having to revise and defend his work, revise it he did—and not to the satisfaction of his modern critics. *Master F. J.* is regarded as Gascoigne's most important work, and almost everyone who has expressed an opinion prefers the first to the revised edition.[15] In the second edition the story becomes simpler from both a moral and a narrative point of view. The moralistic beginning and ending reduce *A Discourse of the Adventures* to a *Fable* warning against lust. Without F. J.'s friend G. T. as narrator the story is clearer, less mysterious, but it has lost the human interest provided by G. T.'s amused sympathy for the adolescent F. J. and partiality for Dame Fraunces. Instead, we are left with the woes of love—F. J. consigned to a life of debauchery, and Fraunces dying from grief at his ingratitude.

Moreover, *Master F. J.* is not the only work to suffer from revision. Perhaps out of a desire to conciliate the Catholic Viscount Montague, who had commissioned a masque and obtained a seat in Parliament for him, Gascoigne revised some lines in "Councell given to master Bartholmew Withipoll." By changing the third "P" which Withipoll is to avoid in Italy from "Papistrie" to "piles and pockes," Gascoigne spoils the climax of the first version, in which poison harms blood and bones, pride poisons body and mind, and

---

[14] I owe this observation about the English names to Gillian Austen, "The Literary Career of George Gascoigne: Studies in Self-Presentation" (Oxford University, D. Phil. thesis, 1996), 151.

[15] Robert P. Adams, "Gascoigne's 'Master *F. J.*' as Original Fiction," *PMLA* 73 (1958): 315; Leicester Bradner, "Point of View in George Gascoigne's Fiction," *Studies in Short Fiction* 3 (1965): 21; Paul Salzman, *An Anthology of Elizabethan Prose Fiction* (Oxford: Oxford Univ. Press, 1987). One partial exception is Walter Davis, *Idea and Act in Elizabethan Fiction* (Princeton: Princeton Univ. Press, 1969), 98.

papistry defiles body and soul with "fouler faultes" (347). In *The Posies* it is not clear in what way "piles and pockes" are worse than poison and pride.

Finally, the division of *The Posies* into "*Floures to comfort, Herbes to cure*, and *Weedes to be avoyded*" (17) serves the moral purpose that Gascoigne outlines in his prefatory letters but is often perplexing in practice. Why, for example, should the translation of the psalm "De profundis" be placed among the more pleasant than profitable flowers instead of the herbs, the moral discourses? Or why should a sequence of six adulterous poems (46–49) or "Dan Bartholmew of Bathe" not join *Master F. J.* among the weeds? One indication of the arbitrariness of some assignments is that "A gloze upon this text, *Dominus iis opus habet*," appears among both the flowers and the weeds. The arrangement of *A Hundreth Sundrie Flowres* as an anthology suits the frankly miscellaneous nature of the collection much better than the moral signposting of *The Posies*.

Desperate for patronage and afraid of giving further offence, Gascoigne gelded *A Hundreth Sundrie Flowres* of more than filthy phrases, and his hints that the new *Master F. J.* is not the translation it purports to be suggest that he felt, at the very least, ambivalent about his revisions. I would like to believe that without external pressure Gascoigne would not have revised his work, but, of course, I cannot be sure of that, since at least a part of Gascoigne—and before 1575—felt some sympathy with the moralizing conception of literature that he uses to organize *The Posies*. Nevertheless, not being able, like an editor of Shakespeare, to print both editions, I have had to choose and have chosen the ungelded edition even though it does not represent Gascoigne's final intentions.

Recent Theoretical Approaches to Editing Renaissance Texts, with Particular Reference to the Folger Library Edition of Hooker's Works

W. SPEED HILL

THE INITIAL PROSPECTUS FOR THE FOLGER LIBRARY EDITION OF Richard Hooker's *Works* was composed Thanksgiving Friday, 1967, and the "Statement of Editorial Policy" is dated June 1, 1970. But its intellectual orgins go back a decade earlier to values inculcated by the graduate English department of Harvard University 1957–1964. The reigning figures in the nondramatic Renaissance there, then, were Douglas Bush, known among the graduate students as Mr. Christian Humanism,[1] and Herschel Baker, author of magisterial surveys of Renaissance intellectual history, *The Dignity of Man* (Cambridge, 1947) and *The Wars of Truth* (Cambridge, 1952).[2] Older presences were Hyder Rollins, editor of Elizabethan poetic miscellanies, and George Lyman Kittridge, editor of Shakespeare. The latter two repre-

---

[1] See *The Renaissance and English Humanism* (Toronto: Univ. of Toronto Press, 1939; rpt. 1941, 1956, 1858, 1962, 1965, and 1968), and *English Literature in the Earlier Seventeenth Century*, 2nd ed. (Oxford: Clarendon Press, 1962).

[2] *The Dignity of Man* was reprinted in paper as *The Image of Man* by Harper in 1961; both were originally printed by Harvard University Press.

sented the older philological tradition, as Baker and Bush represented the
newer mode of intellectual history. Rollins and Baker had recently collaborated on their anthology, *The Renaissance in England* (Boston, 1954). In a tone of
unassailable certitude, they remark that "the great Tudor translations of the
Bible, the Book of Common Prayer, and Hooker's *Of the Laws of Ecclesiastical
Polity* have a timeless beauty" (150). In the same year—and in the same
vein—C. S. Lewis praised Hooker for his having "to our endless joy, [drawn]
out all the tranquil beauty of the old philosophy."[3]

Behind that graduate experience lay four undergraduate years at Princeton
where the New Criticism was the dominant critical mode, available in the
person of R. P. Blackmur, and behind that, three years at Episcopal High
School, where I studied literature from a classic New-Critical text, *An
Approach to Literature* (1952), edited by Robert Penn Warren and Cleanth
Brooks. The dominant editorial theory of the era, the copy-text theories of
W. W. Greg, Fredson Bowers, and G. Thomas Tanselle (I was later to learn)
was rooted in the New-Critical assumptions of the 1950s and '60s, when I
came of textual age, and it flourished in a critical climate that valorized "the
text itself."[4]

Actually, though I was not aware of it at the time, there were *three*
available editorial models in the late 1960s: Documentary editions, Lachmannian stemmatic editions, and Greg–Bowers copy-text editions. But the
reigning mode was copy-text editing: R. B. McKerrow was John the Baptist;
W. W. Greg, Jesus Christ; and Fredson Bowers, St. Paul. Bowers's article,
"Textual Criticism," for the 1963 MLA guide, *The Aims and Methods of Scholarship in Modern Languages and Literatures*, edited by James Thorpe, staked out
his claim to evangelize us textual gentiles. It has thirty-five footnotes: ten cite
Bowers's own writing; an additional twelve draw on his various editorial projects. To be sure, the E.E.T.S. continued to issue its documentary editions; for
example, Clarence Miller's, of Thomas Chaloner's translation of *The Praise of
Folie* (Oxford, 1965) and William A. Ringler's of Sidney's *Poems* (Oxford,
1962), edited in exemplary Lachmannian fashion, but Bowers's self-assumed
role of bibliographical-textual-editorial advocate assured that his views would
dominate debate—as indeed they continue to do in Williams and Abbott's
Introduction to Bibliographical and Textual Studies, published by the MLA in 1985
(2nd ed., 1989).

---

[3] *English Literature of the Sixteenth Century Excluding Drama* (Oxford: Clarendon
Press, 1954), 449.

[4] See D. C. Greetham, "Textual and Literary Theory: Redrawing the Matrix,"
Studies in Bibliography 42 (1989): 1 and n. 3

An anecdote will illustrate Bowers's hegemonic presence. O. B. Hardison, Jr., godfather of the Folger Edition, suggested we sign on Bowers as "Textual Consultant." My nominee, Dick Sylvester, Executive Editor of the Yale St. Thomas More Edition, declined the appointment, pleading that he lacked the qualifications—surely a tribute to Bowers's success in presenting textual criticism as a mystery open only to the bibliographically adept. So I wrote Bowers, who replied that for $1,000 he would vet the editorial principles of the edition, and individual volumes for an additional $1,000 per volume. As none of the contributing editors were being so remunerated, and as I privately regarded his offer as indemnification against one of his notorious slash-and-burn reviews, we rejected his offer. Still, for one educating himself in the editing of vernacular texts in the late 1960s, Bowers' authority—and that of copy-text editing—was pervasive. There really *was* no alternative.

As the actual editing evolved, however, we discovered there *were* alternatives. Books I–IV of the *Lawes* exist as a single printed edition, so, in effect, Georges Edelen's text is a "best-text" edition.[5] My edition of Book V is an orthodox copy-text edition, employing the printer's copy, a scribal transcript corrected by Hooker, as copy-text. However, I had my misgivings at the time as to the adequacy of copy-text theory to the editing of Renaissance texts that exist in manuscript as well as printed forms.[6] Paul Stanwood's texts of Books VI and VIII are products of stemmatic analysis—in the case of Book VIII, a

---

[5] The term is Joseph Bédier's. In 1895 Bédier had first published an edition of the *Lai de L'Ombre* edited according to Lachmannian genealogical procedures. Criticized by Gaston Paris (Bédier's own teacher) for its stemmata, the edition was revised and republished in 1913, with a lengthy preface attacking Lachmannian stemmatic analysis, particularly its tendency to produce two-part (bifid) stemmata. Two later articles published in 1928 set forth his "best text" theory draw on his experience in the two earlier editions, especially as criticized by Paris; see "La tradition manuscrite du *Lai de L'Ombre*: reflexions sur l'art d'editer les anciens textes," *Romania* 54 (1928): 161–196, 321–356; rpt. as pamphlet, 1970. And see Mary Speer, "Old French Literature," *Scholarly Editing: A Guide to Research*, ed. D. C. Greetham (New York: MLA, 1995).

Edelen corrects the text of 1593 in fifty-eight substantives and thirty-two nonsubstantives; in addition, he corrects forty miscitations. Nine substantive corrections and four improvements of punctuation come from two contemporary copies in which manuscript corrections were made: the Wolley copy, in the Pforzheimer Collection (now at the University of Texas, Austin), and Richard Bancroft's copy, in Lambeth Palace Library. See *Folger Library Edition*, 1: xxxi.

[6] See "The Calculus of Error, or Confessions of a General Editor," *Modern Philology* 75 (1978): 247–260.

stemma of some complexity.[7] Laetitia Yeandle's texts of the *Tractates and Sermons* divide between best-text editions of works that survive only in printed exemplars and stemmatic texts of those that survive in multiple manuscript copies. In addition, volumes 3–5 reprint as documents a variety of manuscripts, some newly discovered, such as a set of Autograph Notes relating to the composition of Book VIII, as well as ancillary texts first printed by Keble. In the event, the Hooker Edition became an anthology of editorial methods and models available to the scholarly editor, 1967–1990.

As to "recent theoretical approaches," I would list four: (1) "versioning," where the attempt to conflate various witnesses into a single unified or unitary text is abandoned, and distinct versions, complete in themselves, are reprinted intact, as in the Oxford Shakespeare's printing of both Quarto and Folio *Lears*; (2) a socially based theory of text-production, articulated by Jerome J. McGann in his 1983 *Critique of Modern Textual Criticism*,[8] although ten years later we have as yet no working prototype of a socially edited text;[9] (3) *le texte génétique*, the editing of the full range of authorial drafts without privileging final or published forms of the text—editing texts as process, not product; and (4) the dismissal of all editions not photographic—especially so-called "critical" editions—as *ipso facto* fraudulent.[10]

---

[7] That work survives in ten extant manuscripts and three early printed editions (1648, 1661, 1662). In order to plot them onto a stemma, one must assume the prior existence of six now nonextant manuscripts, or, alternatively, a missing manuscript that was copied and recopied six times before disappearing. See *Folger Library Edition*, 3: li-lxxv, especially the stemma on p. lx.

[8] For an account of its impact, see D. C. Greetham, Foreward, *A Critique of Modern Textual Criticism* (rpt., Charlottesville and London: Univ. of Virginia Press, 1992). For a sample of current [as of 1992] discussion, see Fredson Bowers, "Unfinished Business," *TEXT* 4 (1988): 1–11; Jerome J. McGann, "What is Critical Editing?" and T. H. Howard-Hill, "Theory and Praxis in the Social Approach to Editing" *TEXT* 5 (1991): 15–46 (and McGann, "A Response . . . ," ibid., 47–48); and G. Thomas Tanselle, "Textual Criticism and Literary Sociology," *Studies in Bibliography* 44 (1991): 83–143. McGann's influential *Critique* should be read in conjunction with his 1985 essay, "The Monks and the Giants: Textual and Bibliographical Studies and the Interpretation of Literary Works," in Jerome J. McGann, ed., *Textual Criticism and Literary Interpretation* (Chicago: Univ. of Chicago Press, 1985), 180–199.

[9] Peter Shillingsburg surveys the issues raised by McGann that confront a would-be "social contract editor" in his "Inquiry into the Social Status of Texts and Modes of Textual Criticism," *Studies in Bibliography* 42 (1989): 55–79.

[10] In a variety of articles and lectures, Randall McLeod has demonstrated how pervasive typographic distortion is in any modern letterpress edition. Accordingly, he himself uses only "photoquotes"–photocopied excerpts pasted in his essays—in lieu of typeset quotations, arguing that the best editor is no editor at all. See, for example,

Of these four, two simply do not apply to Hooker. None of Hooker's works survives in forms so distinct as to constitute different versions.[11] Indeed, no Renaissance author's drafts survive in a quantity sufficient to support genetic editing, although I believe the survival of Hooker's Autograph Notes, both for Book VIII and for his answer to the 1599 *A Christian Letter*, is unique for a writer of the period.[12] As for (4), if you think, with Random Cloud, that the best editor is no editor at all, you are not likely to be listening to this paper. In Hooker's case, two facsimiles of Books I–V (but none of Books VI–VIII) became available at the time our edition was going forward: Scolar Press (Menston, 1969) and The English Experience (Amsterdam/New York, 1971), and one of *Two Sermons Upon Part of S. Judes Epistle* (Amsterdam/New York, 1969). Their appeal to start-up graduate programs in English literature is manifest, but neither replaces Keble or, *a fortiori*, the Folger. That leaves us with McGann's social-contract theory. It originates, as Arthur Marotti has observed, in the "cultural materialism . . . implicit in the interpretative practices of the New Historicism,"[13] as expressed in McGann's *Critique* and D. F. McKenzie's *Bibliography and the Sociology of Texts* (1985). But McGann's *Critique* should be read in conjunction with his 1985 essay, "The Monks and the Giants," where he argues (1) that in focusing textual criticism exclusively upon the production of editions, Bowers and Tanselle contributed to the schism between textual criticism and literary interpretation that afflicts

---

"Spellbound," in *Play-Texts in Old Spelling: Papers from the Glendon Conference* [1978], ed. G. B. Shand and Raymond C. Shady (New York: AMS, 1984), 81–96; "Unemending Shakespeare's Sonnet 111," *SEL* 21 (1981): 75–96; "Tranceformations in the Text of *Orlando Furioso*," *New Directions in Textual Studies, The Library Chronicle of the University of Texas at Austin*, 20.1–2 (1990): 61–85; and "Information on Information," *TEXT* 5 (1991): 241–281. Cf. my review of the *New Directions* volume, *TEXT* 6 (1994): 370–381.

For a survey of various editorial models, their histories and their rationales, see my "English Renaissance: Nondramatic Literature," *Scholarly Editing*, 204–230, also available as "Editing Nondramatic Texts of the Renaissance: A Field Guide with Illustrations," the introductory essay in *New Ways of Looking at Old Texts: Papers of the Renaissance English Text Society, 1985–1991*, ed. W. Speed Hill (Binghamton, NY: Medieval & Renaissance Texts & Studies, 1993).

[11] A possible exception would be the tractate *Of Pride*, where the published quarto of 1612 is one-third the length of the Dublin manuscript. However, where the two texts coincide the variants are not revisionary.

[12] See *Folger Library Edition* (Cambridge: Harvard Univ. Press, 1977–1990), 3: 462–538 and 4: 1–81 *passim*, 83–97, and 101–167.

[13] "Manuscript, Print, and the English Renaissance Lyric," *New Ways of Looking at Old Texts*, 210.

the entire profession and (2) that, in adopting the methodology of classical and biblical textual scholarship to the very different conditions of editing "national scriptures," Bowers et al. unduly narrowed the field of view of textual criticism, which McGann defines as "a field of inquiry . . . incumbent upon anyone who works with and teaches literary products," *but* one "that does not meet its fate in the completion of a text of an edition of some particular work."[14]

The real secret of McGann's *Critique* and his subsequent essays is that he is not *really* interested in setting forth a codex-based replacement for copy-text editions. Rather, his energies are directed toward the creation and dissemination of an electronically based hypermedia research archive of "The Complete Writings and Pictures of Dante Gabriel Rossetti."[15] It is intended to occupy, *vis-à-vis* McGann's theorizing, what he asserts the Dekker Edition did for Fredson Bowers or what George Kane and Talbot Donaldson did for *Piers Plowman*: create that oxymoron: a revolutionary scholarly edition. The Oxford Byron did not exemplify McGann's *Critique*: it provoked it. The editorial establishment has taken McGann to task because he has not yet revealed what principle of textual selection would come into play if authorial intention is set aside as the privileged criterion of editorial judgment, but in his published essays McGann has remained outside the range of his critics' fire, concentrating on the revolutionary impact of electronic "editing."

In the absence of specific guidance from McGann—guidance repeatedly and authoritatively offered by Bowers and Tanselle for over a generation—one must infer what a socially determined edition of Richard Hooker might look like.[16]

1. It would not privilege authorial manuscripts, as, for example, the Oxford Shakespeare does not when it bases its text of *Hamlet* on the Folio, not the Second Quarto, which has Shakespeare's autograph behind it. So,

---

[14] "The Monks and the Giants"; see n.8, above. McGann continues: "A proper theory of textual criticism ought to make it clear that we may perform a comprehensive textual and bibliographical study of a work with different ends in view; as part of an editorial operation that will result in the production of an edition; as part of a critical operation for studying the character of that edition; as part of an interpretive operation for incorporating the meaning of the (past) work into a present context. No one of these practical operations is more fundamental than another, and all three depend for their existence on a prior scholarly discipline: textual criticism" (189).

[15] See *TEXT* 7 (1994): 95–105.

[16] An editor who is trying to put McGann's insights into practice is Gerald M. MacLean; see "What is a Restoration Poem? Editing a Discourse, Not an Author," *TEXT* 3 (1985): 319–346.

much of Paul Stanwood's meticulous work on the textual history of the posthumous last three books and Laetitia Yeandle's on that of the *Tractates and Sermons* would inevitably recede in prominence. And I would have opted for the printed text of Book V, which circulated and was read in the seventeenth century as Pullen's scribal transcript was not, although, in my case, the resulting text would not have been materially different from the one we printed.

2. It would attempt to retain the bibliographic codes of the early editions rather than resetting texts in modern typography, even one (Bembo) whose typeface is a modern interpretation of a Renaissance model, either by using photographic facsimiles, or type-facsimiles *à la* Malone Society reprints. But if the former, they would be far less legible, *substituting* the bibliographic code for the linguistic one; if the latter, prohibitively expensive.

3. Most problematically, it would not privilege or foreground Hooker himself; i.e., it would not be an "author-centered" edition. Thus equal space and place would be accorded Thomas Cartwright, Hooker's principal adversary in the *Lawes*, and Walter Travers, Hooker's adversary at the Temple.[17] That would mean reprinting *en bloc* substantial portions of Cartwright's three works,[18] his *Replye* to Whitgift's *Answere*, Whitgift's *Defense of the Aunswere* against Cartwright's *Replye*, Cartwright's *Second Replie* to Whitgift, and Cartwright's *The Reste of the Second Replie*, neither of which Whitgift himself answered. This, in turn, would necessitate reprinting the originary pamphlet in this controversy, the 1572 *Admonition to the Parliament*, to which Whitgift had addressed his *Answere* in 1573. This is exactly what Whitgift himself does in the *Defense*: first, a quote from the *Admonition*, then his response from the *Answere*, then an excerpt from Cartwright's *Replye*, capped by Whitgift's definitive determination, the *Defense* proper—four textual layers in all.[19]

---

[17] Actually, Travers has, since 1612, been accorded a measure of equal billing with Hooker: his *A Supplication made to the Privy Counsel* has traditionally been reprinted with *The Answere of M^r. Richard Hooker to a Supplication Preferred by Mr Walter Travers to the HH. Lords of the Privie Counsell*. See W. Speed Hill, *Richard Hooker: A Descriptive Bibliography of the Early Editions: 1593–1724* (Cleveland and London: The Press of Case Western Reserve Univ., 1970), items 10 and 6.

[18] William P. Haugaard, the commentary editor for the Preface and Books II–IV of the *Lawes*, analyzes Hooker's use of Cartwright, concluding that "Hooker cited 8.9% of the . . . *Replye* . . . 2.6% of . . . *Seconde Replie* and 4.5% of . . . *The Reste of the Second Replie*"; *Folger Library Edition* (Binghamton, NY: Medieval & Renaissance Texts & Studies, 1993), 6: 150.

[19] The growth of the debate can be observed in the illustrations in vol. 6 of *The Folger Library Edition*, 384–392.

Whitgift's *Tractatus 20*, "Of the Authoritie of the Civill Magistrate in Ecclesiasticall matters" occupies pages 694–709. The entire topic occupies Book
VIII of Hooker's *Lawes*, on the royal supremacy. Substantially all of the
Admonition and Whitgift's *Answere* are reprinted in Whitgift's *Defense*. My own
copy of Whitgift is a folio of 823 pages. STC lists two editions. I cannot
believe that the Elizabethan equivalent of the NEH did not subvene the expense of composing, printing, and reprinting this volume, with its complex
multi-layered typography, black-letter, italic, and roman, and its concomitant
changes in font size. Likewise, I cannot believe that the North American
equivalent of Lambeth Palace, the NEH, would subvene its reprinting today,
as the Parker Society did in the 1850s.[20]

Nor would it be sufficient simply to reprint the immediately preceding
controversy: we ought to include Richard Bancroft's two (anonymous)
quartos, *Daungerous positions and proceedings, published and practised within this
Iland of Brytaine, vnder pretence of Reformation, and for the Presbiteriall Discipline*
and *A Survay of the pretended holy discipline. Contayning the beginninges, successe,
parts, proceedings, authority, and doctrine of it: with some of the manifold, and
materiall repugnances, variety, and vncertaineties, in that behalfe. Faithfully gathered,
by way of historicall narration, out of the bookes and writings, of principall fauourers of
that platforme Anno 1593.* To which we should add: John Bridges's *A Defence
of the Gouernment Established in the Church of Englande for Ecclesiasticall Matters.
Contayning an aunswere unto a Treatise called, The Learned Discourse of Eccl.
Government, otherwise intituled, A briefe and plaine declaration concerning the desires
of all the faithfull Ministers, that have, and do seeke for the discipline and reformation
of the Church of Englande. Comprehending likewise an aunswere to the arguments in
a Treatise named The judgement of a most Reverend and Learned man from beyond
the seas, etc. Aunswering also to the argumentes of Calvine, Beza, and Danaeus, with
other our Reverend learned Brethren, besides Caenalis and Bodinus, both for the
regiment of women, and in defence of her Majestie, and of all other Christian Princes
supreme Government in Ecclesiastical causes, Against The Tetrarchie that our Brethren
would erect in every particular congregation, of Doctors, Pastors, Governors and
Deacons, with their severall and joynt authoritie in Elections, Excommunications,
Synodall Constitutions and other Ecclesiasticall matters. Aunswered by John Bridges
Dean of Sarum.*[21] (Bridges' quarto is as long as his title: 1396 pages). To continue to list the relevant titles that make up this particular "discourse" would

---

[20] John Whitgift, *Works*, ed. John Ayre, Parker Society Edition, 46–48 (Cambridge, 1851–1853).

[21] Bancroft's works are STC 1344 and 1352; Bridges' is 3734; he is replying to
William Fulke (STC 10395) and Hadrian Saravia (STC 2021).

only induce hypnosis. Other, younger and more energetic, more politically astute scholars may see gold where I see dross; perhaps we have the making of yet another Garland Archive here. To be sure, by burying excerpts of Bridges, Bancroft, Whitgift, Cosin, Bilson, Sutcliffe, Saravia, Fulke, Cartwright, Travers, Jewel, et al. in our (still quite full) annotations, we subordinate them to Hooker, but that, after all, has been the verdict of history, which has kept Hooker in print for most of the four hundred years since 1593, while allowing his confrères and antagonists to gather dust on rare-book shelves.[22]

The politically correct will say: "but the established Church suppressed *The Admonition*, the *Second Admonition*, and the first edition of Cartwright's *Replye*—the formal censorship of books in Elizabethan England being delegated to the Bishop of London. By centering your edition on Hooker, you are simply recapitulating that original suppression and so compounding an earlier injustice." All true. But if you want the Folger's name on your edition, if you want the NEH to pay its editorial and publication costs, if you want Harvard University Press to publish it, you do not interrogate history's verdict too vigorously. From Henry Hallam in 1827, who described Hooker as a knight of romance among the vulgar brawlers of religious controversy,[23] to H. R. Trevor-Roper in 1977,[24] not to speak of the celebratory prose of my contributing editors, Hooker's *Lawes* has historically been accorded an exceptional status, being admitted to the canon of English *literature*, as it was at Harvard a generation ago, as a literary *work*, not a mere historical *document*.[25]

----

[22] Cartwright's *Replye* went into an immediate second edition, doubtless because the first was ordered suppressed, but apart from its incorporation in the Parker Society's edition of Whitgift's *Defense* (equivalent to his *Works*), it has never been reprinted since 1574.

[23] *The Constitutional History of England from the Accession of Henry VII to the Death of George II*, 5th ed. (London, 1846), 1: 214, first published in 1827.

[24] Speaking at the publication of volumes 1 and 2 of the Edition, Trevor–Roper remarked on Hooker's "Olympian" reputation, seeming to stand so "benignly above the battle in which, historically, he had been so deeply engaged" (103), and concluded by quoting Lord Acton, testimony that "in the sixteenth century . . . as a serious quest for a set of principles which should hold good alike under all changes of religion, 'Hooker's *Ecclesiastical Polity* stands almost alone.' " See "Richard Hooker and the Church of England," *Renaissance Essays* (Chicago: Univ. of Chicago Press, 1985), first printed in the *New York Review of Books*, 24 November 1977.

[25] For example, the Pforzheimer Collection, English Literature 1475–1640, has five Hooker items (498–502) but no other works of Elizabethan religious controversy. *Of the Lawes of Ecclesiasticall Politie* was included in the exhibition, *Printing and the Mind of Man* (London and New York, 1967)—i.e., as one of the hundred most important books of the modern West. Citing a 1930 Cornell dissertation by Lewis Freed, "The Sources of Johnson's Dictionary," Alvin Kernan notes that, after Locke, Hooker was

In retrospect, it is clear to me that a scholarly edition is not as exempt from the contingencies of the time and place in which it is undertaken as earlier I had naively assumed, and I am quite sure that an edition of Hooker's *Works* could not be mounted on the scale of the Folger Library Edition were it to be inaugurated today. The auspices were unusually favorable twenty-five years ago; they seem distinctly less so today.[26] The authority of the author-centered critical edition as a scholarly ideal has all but disappeared, at least among textualists.[27] The literary canon into which Hooker was atypically inserted is itself being reconstituted. "Literature" in the traditional sense is suspect,[28] and both "timeless beauty" and "the tranquil beauty of the old philosophy" are being remaindered. But, if you deny Hooker his exceptionalism, you undercut as well the profession's support for the editing of his works, and

---

the second most quoted author in the first volume of the *Dictionary*, with 1,212 citations; *Samuel Johnson and the Impact of Print* (Princeton: Princeton Univ. Press, 1989), 196, first published in 1987 as *Printing Technology, Letters, and Samuel Johnson*. And excerpts from the *Lawes* still grace the two standard anthologies in the field, Norton and Oxford; *The Norton Anthology of English Literature*, 2 vols., 6th ed., M. H. Abrams, gen. ed. (New York, 1993), 1: 1013–1020, and *The Oxford Anthology of English Literature*, 2 vols., ed. Frank Kermode and John Hollander (New York, 1973), 1: 1424–1429. Most telling of all, both the New and the "Old" *Cambridge Bibliography of English Literature* accord Hooker a section to himself (§4.VI), thus ranking him with Chaucer (§2.III), Milton (§2.VI), and Shakespeare (§3.IX), the only other authors so singled out.

On the distinction between "text" and "work," see G. Thomas Tanselle, *A Rationale of Textual Criticism* (Philadelphia: Univ. of Pennsylvania Press, 1989), and Margreta de Grazia, "What is a Work? What is a Document," *New Ways of Looking at Old Texts*, 199–207.

[26] See "Editing Richard Hooker: A Retrospective," *Sewanee Theological Review* 36.2 (Easter 1993): 187–199.

[27] See my review of *New Directions in Textual Studies* (1989), *The Library Chronicle of the University of Texas at Austin*, 20.1–2 (1990), in *TEXT* 6 (1994): 370–382, as well as that of D. C. Greetham, "Enlarging the Text," in *Review* 14 (1992): 1–33. See also my review of *Palimpsest: Editorial Theory in the Humanities*, ed. George Bornstein and Ralph G. Williams (Ann Arbor: Univ. of Michigan Press, 1993), for *Yeats: An Annual of Critical and Textual Studies*, 12 (1996 for 1994): 261–276. See also, *inter alia*, Derek Pearsall, "Revision and Revisionism in Middle English Editing," forthcoming, *TEXT* 7 (1994): 107–126; and Stephen Orgel, "Prospero's Wife," *Representing the English Renaissance*, ed. Stephen Greenblatt (Berkeley: Univ. of California Press, 1988), 219–220. Orgel was a speaker at the 1988 Toronto Conference on Editorial Problems, aptly entitled, "Crisis in Editing: Texts of the English Renaissance," which canvassed just such topics (ed. Randall McLeod [New York: AMS, 1994]).

[28] See Alvin Kernan, *The Death of Literature* (New Haven: Yale Univ. Press, 1990).

you are truly left with a "University Carrier's" choice: an edition erected on what are rapidly becoming obsolete textual assumptions, an edition erected on more current ideological assumptions but prohibitively expensive to produce and stupifyingly dull to read, or no edition at all. I take my stand by the first of these alternatives.

Robert Burton's Sources
and Late Topical Revision in
The Anatomy of Melancholy

THOMAS C. FAULKNER

NOW THAT THE THIRD AND FINAL VOLUME OF THE TEXT OF Robert Burton's *The Anatomy of Melancholy* is complete, with the two commentary volumes due to follow in about two years, it is appropriate to discuss two of the ways the new Clarendon Edition will open up new approaches to the *Anatomy*. The first of these is the record of the growth of the *Anatomy* provided by the textual apparatus, and the second is the accurate identification of many of Burton's sources for the first time.

Apart from the correction of compositor's errors, and the major contribution of the forthcoming commentary, the greatest assistance the Clarendon Edition of the *Anatomy* will provide to Burton scholarship is the identification of the editions in which the thousands of added passages originate. This permits the tracking of Burton's reading and the development of his ideas during the course of the six editions, through which the work expanded from 353,369 words in 1621 to 516,384 words in 1651. Scholars have long been interested in analyzing Burton's progressive development of various topics through the growing *Anatomy*. Lawrence Babb devoted a chapter of *Sanity in Bedlam: A Study of Robert Burton's* Anatomy of Melancholy (East Lansing, 1959) to an analysis of the growth of six passages. Earlier J. Max Patrick wrote about the development of Burton's concept of the ideal commonwealth in "Robert Burton's Utopianism" (*PQ* 27, 1948). And Robert M. Browne has traced the evolution of Burton's cosmology in "Robert Burton and the New

Cosmology" (*MLQ* 13, 1952). However, all previous efforts to discuss the growth of the *Anatomy* have been limited to specific sections because there has never been a complete collation of all six editions. Dennis G. Donovan undertook a collation of "Religious Melancholy" for his 1965 University of Illinois dissertation, but his analysis consists principally of lists of authors added in each edition.

"Religious Melancholy" provides good examples of Burton's revisions made in response to the changing political and religious climate of the 1630s. What is most significant about Burton's additions to this section in 1632 and 1638 is the sharpening of his attacks on non-Christian religions, Catholicism, and the English Puritans. In other words, he strengthens the case for the Church of England in the midst of increasing pressure from the noncon-formists that culminated in the Civil Wars that began the year after Burton's death. Of course, Burton's anti-Catholicism pervades the *Anatomy* and was consistent throughout his life, but in "Religious Melancholy" he reinforces the identification of Catholicism with paganism—a thesis central to the reformers' criticism of the Catholic church. With consummate irony he introduces in 1638 José de Acosta's account of the pagan practices at the time of the conquest of the Americas in *Historia natural y moral de las Indias* (Seville, 1590), translated by Edward Grimstone as *The Naturall and Morall Historie of the East and West Indies* (London, 1604):

> what strange Sacraments, like ours of Baptisme and the Lords Supper, what goodly Temples, Priests, sacrifices they had in *America* when the *Spaniards* first landed there, let *Acosta* the Jesuite relate *lib. 5. cap. 1, 2, 3, 4,* &c. and how the Divel imitated the Arke, and the children of *Israels* comming out of *Egypt;* with many such. (3.345: 5–9. All references are to volume, page, and line numbers in the Clarendon Edition)

In 1632 he quoted the following passage from Sir Edward Sandys, *A Relation of the State of Religion,* originally published in 1605, but reissued in 1629: "*The worst Christians of Italy are the Romans, of the Romans the Priests are leudest, the leudest priests are preferred to be Cardinalls, & the baddest man amongst the Cardinalls is chosen to be Pope*" (3.351: 12–14). A page later Burton added the following quotation from John Speed's *The Theater of the Empire of Great Britain* (the publication of a new edition in 1631 may have brought Speed back to Burton's notice):

> We have had in *England,* as *Armachanus* demonstrates, above thirty thousand Friers at once; & as *Speed* collects out of *Lelande* and others, almost 600 religious houses, and neere two hundred thousand pound in revenewes of the old rent, belonging to them, besides Images of

Gold, Silver, plate, furniture, goods and ornaments, as *Weever* calcu-
lates and esteems them at the dissolution of Abbies, worth a million of
gold. (3.352: 18–24)

Other late additions to Burton's polemic include references to and quotations
from Tommaso Campanella, *Atheismus triumphatus, sive reductio ad religionem per
scientiarum veritates* (Rome, 1631) against atheists; Jacobus Boissardus, *De Divi-
natione & Magicis Praestigiis* (1616) against paganism; and Theodorus Biblian-
der's treatise on the Alcoran appended to his edition of a twelfth-century Latin
translation.

An excellent example of how the *Anatomy* deals with contemporary events
is Burton's treatment of the Sabbatarian controversy. This long-standing controversy between Puritans and Anglicans over the observance of Sunday had
caused James I to issue in 1618 a declaration authorizing rural sports following
divine service. This declaration, known as the Book of Sports, was reissued by
Charles I on October 18, 1633, in response to increasing Puritan attempts to
put down Sunday rural sports. In the declaration, the King specifically authorizes Sunday afternoon recreations that various Puritan local authorities had
banned:

Our pleasure likewise is, that the bishop of that diocesse [Chester]
take the like straight order with all the Puritans and Precisians within
the same, either constraining them to conforme themselves, or to
leave the countrey according to the laws of our kingdome and canons
of our church, and so to strike equally on both hands against the con-
temners of our authority and adversaries of our church. And as for our
good people's lawfull recreation, our pleasure likewise is, that, after the
end of divine service, our good people be not disturbed, letted, or
discouraged from any lawfull recreation, such as dauncing, either men
or women, archerie for men, leaping, vaulting, or any other such
harmlesse recreations, nor from having of May-games, Whitsun ales,
and Morris-dances, and the setting up of May-poles, and other sports
therewith used, so as the same be had in due and convenient time,
without impediment or neglect of divine service; and that women
shall have leave to carry rushes to the church for the decoring of it,
according to their old custome. But withall we doe here accompt still
as prohibited all unlawfull games to be used upon Sundays only, as
beare and bull baitings, interludes, and at all times in the meaner sort
of people, by law prohibited, bowling. (*Somers Tracts*, 2: 55)

As the Book of Sports was ordered to be read in all churches, Burton would
have first read it in 1618 at St. Thomas's in Oxford where he had been vicar
since November 1616 when he was presented by the Dean and Chapter of

Christ Church. When it was reissued by Charles I in 1633, Burton would have again read it at St. Thomas's and would have seen to it that his curate, John Mallinson, read the declaration in his living of Seagrave in Leicestershire, which he held from 15 June 1632.

Burton first dealt with the Sabbatarian controversy in the "Exercise Rectified" subsection of the 1621 edition of the *Anatomy*. Here in the context of recommending healthy exercise as a remedy for melancholy, he attacks the Puritan attempts to prohibit rural sports and entertainments on Sunday:

> *Dancing, Singing, Masking, Mumming, Stage-plaies,* howsoever they bee heavily censured by some severe *Catoes,* yet if opportunely & soberly used, may justly be approved. *Melius est fodere, quàm saltare,* saith *Austin,* but what is that if they delight in it? *Nemo saltat sobrius,* But in what kinde of dance? I knowe these sports have many oppugners, whole Volumes writ against them; and some againe, because they are now cold and wayward, past themselves, cavell at all such youthfull sports in others, as he did in the Comedy, they thinke them, *Illicò nasci senes &c.* [Terence, *Heautontimorumenos* 213] Some out of preposterous zeale object many times triviall arguments, and because of some abuse, will quite take away the good use, as if they should forbid wine, because it makes men drunk; but in my judgement they are too sterne: there is a time for all things, for my part, I will subscribe to the *Kings Declaration,* and was ever of that mind, those May-games, wakes, & Whitson-ales, &c. if they be not at unseasonable houres, may justly be permitted. (2.82: 1–17)

In 1628 Burton added the next sentence: "Let them freely feast, sing & dance, have their poppet playes, hobby-horses, tabers, croudes, bag-pipes &c. play at ball, and barley-breakes, & what sports and recreations they like best" (2.82: 17–19).

Burton's additions to "Religious Melancholy" in the 1638 edition of the *Anatomy* reflect the recent intensification of the Sabbatarian controversy. In the "Symptoms of Religious Melancholy" subsection, he specifically added "hawking, hunting, &c." (3.387: 9–10) as examples of "honest recreations" prohibited by the Puritans. A few pages later he added "hauking, hunting, singing, dancing" to the enumeration of "many good and lawfull things, honest disports, pleasures and recreations" created by God "for our use" (3.391: 9–10). And a few lines later he adds this passage:

> So that he that will not rejoyce and enjoy himselfe, making good use of such things as are lawfully permitted, *non est temperatus,* as he will, *sed superstitiosus. There is nothing better for a man, than that hee should eat and drinke, and that hee should make his Soule enjoy good in his labour,*

Eccles. 2. 24. And as one said of hauking and hunting, *tot solatia in hac ægri orbis calamitate mortalibus tædiis Deus objecit,* I say of all honest rec-reations, God hath therefore indulged them to refresh, ease, solace and comfort us. (3.391: 15–22)

A few lines below, Burton adds "honest sports, games, and pleasant recrea-tions" as examples of "many good gifts" which Puritans seek to deprive the people of because they "tyrannize over our brothers soules" (3.391: 27–28). Finally, at the bottom of page 391, Burton recounts a scurrilous thirteenth-century anecdote from Sebastian Munster about a Jew who fell into a privy on the sabbath and was unable to be rescued on Saturday because of Jewish sabbatarianism or on Sunday because of Christian sabbatarianism. Unfortu-nately the man died before Monday. Clearly Burton was not aiming primarily at thirteenth-century Jews or Christians, but at seventeenth-century Sabbatar-ians, as he makes clear by observing that "Wee have myriads of examples in this kind" and adding in 1632 "amongst those rigid Sabbatarians."

He was still concerned with the Sabbatarian controversy when he last re-vised "Exercise Rectified" for the posthumous 1651 edition. He expanded the quotation from Ecclesiastes, adding, *"a time to mourne, a time to dance. Eccles. 3. 4. a time to embrace, a time not to embrace, (vers. 5) and nothing better then that a man should rejoyce in his own works. vers. 22"* (2.82: 12–14). Thus in these late additions to "Religious Melancholy" and "Exercise Rectified," Burton up-holds the Laudian Erastianism of the Book of Sports and castigates the Puritans for their Sabbatarianism.

Perhaps the most persistent editorial problem in editing *The Anatomy of Melancholy* is accurate identification of Burton's citations and quotations. The large number of such references is, of course, a major part of the problem. We have 2,419 entries in our indexes of historical persons, the majority of whom are authors cited or quoted by Burton.

The frequently stated opinion that Burton is inaccurate and careless in his quotations and references often proves to be unfounded when Burton's speci-fic source for a given quotation is discovered. From the start of the Clarendon Edition, Burton's own library has been of considerable assistance in estab-lishing the source of quotations and citations for about half of his authorities. My colleague Nicolas Kiessling, in *The Library of Robert Burton* (Oxford Bib-liographical Society, 1988), has catalogued 1,738 books Burton once owned, of which all but 210 are in the Bodleian or Christ Church libraries. However, there is no record that Burton owned the works of some of his most fre-quently quoted authors (Ariosto, Aristotle, Arnobius, Augustine, Timothy Bright, Jerome Cardan, Joannes Heurnius, Horace, Joannes Baptista Mon-tanus, Plato, and Victorius Trincavellius, for example); he often quoted from

editions other than those he owned; his citations for Greek works typically are
to Latin versions, and his references to and quotations from the works of
various authors are frequently from what we today call "through references"—
anthologies like Erasmus's *Adagia*.

A good example of his use of anthologies, from the subsection "Cure of
Love Melancholy," is found on page 245 of the third volume. Here in a catalogue of unrequited love, Burton quotes from several eclogues, but cites only
"Erasmus Egl. Galatea" in note d at line 21. However, only lines 26–27 were
found in the eclogue Galatea in the 1540 edition of Erasmus's *Omnia Opera*
published in Basel by Froben. *"Despectus tibi sum,"* in line 24 is from Virgil,
Ecl. 2.19. The source of lines 20–23 was ultimately found in an anthology of
pastoral verse in the Bodleian that was part of Burton's library. The item,
Kiessling 242, is entitled *Bucolicorum autores XXXVIII. Quotquot videlicet a Ver-
gilii aetate ad nostra usque tempora* ... (Basel, 1546). Here the line "Cautibus
Ismariis immotior," which Burton paraphrases as "hard as flint," is found
in another version of the eclogue entitled "Pamphilus sive Eros," and here too
we have located sources for Burton's quotations from other pastorals, for
example, Mantuan's first eclogue "Faustus"—the eclogue most frequently
quoted in the *Anatomy*.

Another difficult problem is the references Burton makes to works that are
complementary or explanatory to other works from which he is directly quoting. When such references are garbled, they can be extremely difficult to
identify. An example may be seen in a passage on pages 369–370 from the
third volume. Burton here cites a list of rational objections to the Christian
religion and its sacraments compiled by Tommaso Campanella in his *Atheismus
Triumphatus* (1631). Christianity, Campanella says, "is a most difficult dogma,
subject to the blasphemies of heretics and the derision of politicians" who
hold it impossible that "God is eaten as bread" and scoff at the absurdity of
the sacrament, arguing that "God is ridiculed by worms and flies when they
pollute and devour him: he is subject to fire, water and robbers. They throw
down the golden pix, yet this God does not defend himself. How is he able
to remain entire when the host is in so very many pieces, in the sky, on the
earth, etc." At the beginning of this last passage, added in 1638, as were all of
the references to Campanella's *Atheismus Triumphatus,* Burton has a marginal
note "Lege Hossman: Mus exenteratus" (370: v). After a long and futile search
for the reference in works by Hossman (Abraham Hossmanus) or Daniel
Hoffman, the correct source of the citation was finally located in Rodolphus
Hospinianus's *Historia sacramentaria* (1598–1602). Hospinian, a Swiss Protestant
theologian, takes aim at the ritualistic absurdities of the Catholic sacraments.
Burton's citation refers to Hospinian's explanation of the problem of what is
to be done if a mouse eats the consecrated host. The answer is, if you can

catch the mouse, you kill it, disembowel it (Mus exenteratus), rescue any bits of the bread that have survived, burn the mouse, bowels, and bread, and lay the ashes reverently on the altar.

Burton's intention is clear: the ritualistic and pagan absurdities of Catholics are just as ridiculous as the skeptical criticism of the sacraments made by atheists. Or, in Burton's words: "But he that shall read the *Turks Alcoran,* the *Jewes Talmud,* and Papists *Golden Legend,* in the meane time will sweare that such grosse fictions, fables, vaine traditions, prodigious paradoxes and ceremonies, could never proceed from any other spirit, then that of the divell himselfe, which is the Author of confusion and lies" (370: 6–10).

A third example of a troublesome source problem is found in the quotation from Marinus Marsennus found in the second volume on page 53 at note e. Referring to those who complain of "moderne Divines" (presumably Scholastic theologians and apologists for the Counter-Reformation, but probably also skeptical Anglicans like Burton himself) who "are too severe and rigid against Mathematitians; ignorant and peevish, in not admitting their true demonstrations and certaine observations, that they tyrannize over arte, science, and all philosophy, in suppressing their labours, . . . forbidding them to write, to speake a truth, all to maintaine their superstition, and for their profits sake," Burton quotes from Marsennus's *Quaestiones Celeberrimae in Genesim* (Paris, 1623): "Now they persuade theologians to remain in the greatest ignorance, to be unwilling to accept true knowledge, and to exert tyranny, so that they can keep them in false dogmas, superstitions and the Catholic religion." However, this passage is only found in some copies, the leaf having been canceled apparently to avoid attracting the attention of the Inquisition. The cancellandum (Sig. e) is present in the Bodleian copy, but the Christ Church copy has the cancallans.

These three example of problems in locating accurate sources of Burton's citations and quotations in the *Anatomy* provide an insight into why it has taken Rhonda Blair, Nicolas Kiessling and me over a decade to complete work on the text and why John Bamborough required another three years to ready the commentary for publication.

On Representing Tyndale's English

ANNE RICHARDSON

I DELIVERED A DRAFT OF THIS PAPER AT THE 1993 SESSION OF THE Modern Language Association—on the eve of William Tyndale's 500th year, when his reputation had vaulted into a triumphal phase. A scholar not given to exaggeration had said of the heresiarch that he "wrote like an angel; no English writer has had such influence while remaining so unrecognized."[1] In allusion to Tyndale's biblical translations, a bold epigram made the rounds: "What William Shakespeare did for English poetry, William Tyndale did for English prose."[2] The year 1994 saw two new books on Tyndale,[3] two international conferences, and well-attended exhibits, notably at the British Library and the Tyndale Museum at Vilvoorde, Belgium. Memorial services were held in churches throughout the English-speaking world (including Archbishop Desmond Tutu's Capetown), in which readings from the Bible were in Tyndale's versions. An international Tyndale Society was founded, charged with sponsoring two journals, one a fresh forum for members' ideas, the other a scholarly annual.

---

[1] Excerpt from a review by M. A. Screech in the London *Times,* quoted in an undated flyer issued in October 1992 by Yale University Press, London.

[2] It was printed in modified form in the Newsletter of the William Tyndale Quincentenary Committee in October 1992.

[3] David Daniell, *William Tyndale: A Biography* (New Haven and London: Yale Univ. Press, 1994), and *William Tyndale and the Law,* ed. John A. R. Dick and Anne Richardson, *Sixteenth Century Essays and Studies* 25 (Kirksville, MO: Sixteenth Century Journal Publishers, 1994).

For all that, there is still no consensus on Tyndale; at least, nothing that has hardened into dogma. John Fines regards Tyndale as the sole, indispensable force behind the English Reformation.[4] Richard Marius denies him that supreme causality, but proposes 1525, the year in which Tyndale succeeded in printing the first fragment of his New Testament, as the beginning of the modern era.[5] Certainly to an unquiet England Tyndale gave powerful thought, including a nascent formulation of the prescriptive human rights that serve as touchstones of civil behavior in our time.[6]

He was congenial with our concerns in other ways. By comparison with most of his contemporaries, he was a pacifist;[7] by comparison, a feminist;[8] and again by comparison, an advocate for religious toleration in a world engorged with *odium theologicum* and its violent subaltern, antisemitism.[9] These modernities no less than his theological allegiances swept Tyndale to the stake. It is astonishing that a person who led such a menaced life could write with joyous tenderness. The following translation of the Song of Solo-

---

[4] *Biographical Register of Early English Protestants: 1525–1558*, 2 vols. (London, 1980–1987), unpaginated.

[5] *Thomas More: A Biography* (New York: Random House, 1984), 311.

[6] See Leonard W. Levy, *Origins of the Fifth Amendment: The Right against Self-Incrimination*, 2nd ed. (New York: Collier Macmillan, 1986): 62–64; and Anne Richardson, "William Tyndale and the Bill of Rights," *William Tyndale and the Law*, 11–29.

[7] He was an Erasmian pacifist well past the 1526 Siege of Mohacs, an event which moved Erasmus himself, in *De bello turcico*, to compromise his own pacifism by admitting the notion of a just war. Tyndale later modified his own views on war and physical violence. See *An Answer to Sir Thomas More's Dialogue . . .*, ed. Henry Walter (Cambridge: Cambridge Univ. Press for the Parker Society, 1850), 188; and *Expositions and Notes on Sundry Portions of the Holy Scriptures, together with The Practice of Prelates*, ed. Henry Walter (ibid., 1849), 63, 67.

[8] If a reasonable criterion for male feminism is a man's toleration or advocacy of women's performance in traditionally male roles, Tyndale (anachronistically) fits the bill. In his controversy with More over ordination, Tyndale (with certain exceptions) follows Paul's prohibition of women preachers, but infuriates More by pronouncing women qualified to perform the sacraments and considers "widow," for a woman of 60 or older, as an office of the church (*An Answer*, 18, 29–30, 98, 176).

[9] The only wholehearted advocate for the rights of Jews in Tyndale's Europe was Johannes Reuchlin (1455–1522). Tyndale less passionately believed that Jews had the natural law right to live in peace. He denounced the violence of his fellow Christians: "We be taught even of very babes / to kyll a turke / to slee a Jewe / to burne an heretike . . ." (*The Obedience of a Christian Man*, STC 24446 [Antwerp: Johan Hoochstraten, 1528], sig. C7v/7–9). Subsequent citations from the *Obedience* will give signature and line numbers, as here.

mon 2, shaped for presentation as a liturgical epistle, accompanied Tyndale's 1534 revised New Testament:

> I am the floure of the felde, and lylyes of the valeyes. As the lylye amonge the thornes, so is my loue amonge the daughters. As the appletre amonge the trees of the wood so is my beloued amonge the sonnes: in his shadow was my desyer to syt, for his frute was swete to my mouth. He brought me into his wyne seller: and his behauer to mewarde was louely. Beholde my beloued sayde to me: vp and hast my loue, my doue, my bewtifull and come, for now is wynter gone and rayne departed and past. The floures apere in our contre and the tyme is come to cut the vynes. The voyce of the turtle doue is harde in oure lande. The fygge tre hath brought forth her fygges, and the vyne blossoms geue a sauoure. Vp hast my loue, my doue, in the holes of the rocke and secret places of the walles. Shew me thy face and let me here thy voyce, for thy voyce is swete and thy fassyon bewtifull.[10]

Such loveliness is the best argument for representing Tyndale's English in our national university curriculum. In particular, to experiment with Tyndale's "ravishing solo"[11] as the base text replacing the various bibles-by-committee for a course in the Bible as literature might free up good energies. We are unaccustomed to humor, to sprightliness in our experience of Holy Writ. The history of English Christianity might have developed quite differently, had Tyndale mediated its sacred book.

We proceed to the comic crux of Gen. 3:1–4, in which the serpent clears his throat and accosts Eve in the masculine honorific as "syr."

> Ah syr, that God hath sayd, ye shal not eate of all maner trees in the garden. And the woman sayd vnto the serpent, of the frute of the trees in the garden we may eate, but of the frute that is in the middes of the garden (sayd God) se that ye eat not, and se that ye touch it

---

[10] Tyndale included in an appendix to his 1534 New Testament this and other Old Testament passages adaptable to liturgical use. I quote this passage in its original spelling from *The New Testament translated by William Tyndale (1534) ... with ... the variants of the edition of 1525 [–1526]*, ed. N. Hardy Wallis (Cambridge: Cambridge Univ. Press, 1938), 580. This and other Old Testament liturgical epistles are also available with modernized accidentals in *Tyndale's New Testament translated from the Greek by William Tyndale in 1534*, ed. David Daniell (London and New Haven: Yale Univ. Press, 1989).

[11] David Daniell, *Tyndale's New Testament*, vii.

not: lest ye dye. Then sayd the serpent vnto the woman: tush ye shall not dye.[12]

Can Tyndale be telling us that the prelapsarian Satan has not yet got the cosmos figured out? He sees that this pair of creatures are different from himself (and most unwelcome), but fails to note that they are different from each other!

The crux lies in the likelihood that Tyndale, elated by the comic possibilities of this scene, threw to the winds the Erasmian ideas of going *ad fontes* to the Hebrew, and his own excellence in the *trilinguum*, and with "Ah syr" playfully improvised. According to Gerald Hammond, the original Hebrew expression which "Ah syr" is meant to translate, *af ki* (in informal notation), is unique here in the Old Testament. It has the force of an incredulous query: "Did God *really* say ... ?"[13]—or as John Rogers, editor of the 1537 "Matthew" Bible (STC 2066) re-Hebraized the verse: "Ye, hath God sayd in dede ... ?" Attempts to integrate this ironical "indeed" by interpreting "syr" as "sure" or "surely" are defeated by the absence of any lexicographic record of such use.[14] The housewifely "apurns" that the delinquent couple sew for themselves at the end of the episode provide another comic touch. No reference book I have consulted on *aprons* says that they cover more than the front of the body.

I close this argument for Tyndale's inclusion in the canon by reporting a colleague's repeated use of the great exordium ("William Tyndale other wise called William Hychins vnto the Reader") of *The Obedience of a Christian Man* as an introductory assignment in her course in sixteenth-century English literature. Her classes were increasingly made up of people from countries in which human rights were routinely violated. There was no Tyndalian theme, from censorship to martyrdom, that left them uncomprehending or unmoved. Many voted this first assignment their favorite reading of the year.

Is it necessary to defend modernizing of accidentals? This is needed by the

---

[12] William Tyndale, *The firste boke of Moses*, rev. ed., STC 2351 (Antwerp: M. de Keyser, 1534), sig. B2v. Tyndale's translation of Genesis first appeared with the whole of the Pentateuch in 1530 (STC 2350).

[13] Gerald Hammond, letter to the author, 8 December 1993. J. H. Hertz, in *The Pentateuch and Haftorahs*, five vols. (London: Oxford Univ. Press, 1929), 1:25, translates, "Is it really so, that God (Elohim) hath said?"

[14] Hammond's point; also see David Daniell, *William Tyndale*, 407 nn. 1–3. Hammond further suggests consulting the *OED* for *sirrah*: it is "first recorded in the 1520's; used playfully in addressing men or women; and, according to one authority, the suffixal part of it may be derived from the interjection, 'ah!' So, is it possible that 'Ah syr' = 'Sir ah?'"

readership of literate generalists we would be foolish to patronize. I especially endorse David Daniell's policy, in his modern-spelling editions of Tyndale's scripture texts,[15] of honoring Tyndale's light punctuation, which we may experience as underpunctuation. Tyndale, a fabled linguist, often prefers rhythm and word order to punctuation marks. An analogy might be made to the elegant frugality of the water colorist who indicates white in an area by leaving the paper blank. By contrast, the only currently available source of Tyndale's polemical and other independent writings—the Parker Society edition of 1848–1850—by overpunctuation direly misrepresents Tyndale's English for modern readers. The commas and semicolons are fussy. Worse, the nonauthorial exclamation points turn up the sound in a most unpleasant way. Tyndale, self-fashioned as a friend speaking to friends, is in such a presentation as alienating as a religious fanatic haranguing a crowd of the converted: Savonarola in a cold climate.

But all sound modernization must rest on an attempt at representation of what Tyndale actually wrote. My own store of such particulate matter derives not from the biblical translations but from work on a critical edition of *The Obedience of a Christian Man*, originally presented in 1976.[16] In such an enterprise, it scarcely needs saying that one feels the pull of extremes between the authoritarian approach that rejects all elements of Tyndale's text not given entries in the *Oxford English Dictionary* or the *Middle English Dictionary*, and an antinomianism so casual as to grant mere printers' errors the status of words in Tyndale's text.

This customary editorial dilemma is sharpened by a triad of Tyndale-specific conditions: our insufficient lexicographic control of the diction of Tyndale and his Early Tudor contemporaries; Tyndale's need, as a renegade English cleric, to entrust his writings to underground printers and their staffs; and the role in Tyndale's written language of the non-standard phonology of speech and writing in the Welsh border country of his birth.

Trusting lexicographic aids is a delicate matter in the case of any of the early reformers—or of those with whom they locked horns. In the bibliographical portion of the Supplement of the *OED* it is revealed that, gamely, the team of lexicographers compiled their findings from the original editions of all texts by Tyndale and by John Frith. But for Thomas More's spellings they

---

[15] Daniell's 1989 edition of Tyndale's 1534 New Testament edition was followed by *Tyndale's Old Testament* (London and New Haven: Yale Univ. Press, 1992), which contains the Pentateuch, Joshua through 2 Chronicles and Jonah. This is approximately one-half of the Old Testament, translated by Tyndale before his arrest in 1535.

[16] "A Critical Edition of William Tyndale's *The Obedience of a Christian Man*," Ph.D. diss., Yale University, 1976.

used the normalized 1557 *Works*, published some twenty-two years after More's execution. And in the case of that amusing rascal, Dr. Robert Barnes, finally brought down in 1540 along with his protector Thomas Cromwell, all citations of his writings were taken from the Daye–Foxe 1572 *Whole Works* of the Reformers, a landmark in systematic normalization. A search of the *OED* Supplement since delivery of this paper in 1993 reveals good selective coverage of Tyndale's fellow-reformers.[17] But there is not the corroborative pool of actual forms and spellings in the epoch of 1525–1550 that would enable a lexicographer to eye a dubious vocable and confidently pronounce it not a typo but a word.

For example, in the *Obedience* we find two uses of *o* for *a*: *obove, onoynted*. For the first, the *OED* has only *obowen*—traced to the north of England and time-centered in the fourteenth century. Moving to the *MED*, which is excellent company to Tyndalians in its documentation of the Lollard presence—see the definition of *to loll [someone]*—we find both *obove* and *onoynt*. However, in accordance with the self-imposed guidelines of the *MED*, we are not given a region of England or the time of a given word's entrance into the language before the cutoff of coverage in 1475. James L. Harner recommends consulting the *MED* in tandem with McIntosh's linguistic atlas,[18] which in its cartographic splendor of four folio volumes has the potential of great precision in corroborating a Tyndale spelling. But Harner remarks that the Atlas is difficult to use. Indeed, its size and weight impede frequent—and clearly essential—cross-references between the volumes. A source still in development for Tyndale's words and his antedatings to the *OED*'s entries is the Michigan Early Modern English Materials (MEMEM).[19] The most exciting development in the way of firming our lexicographic grip on Tyndale's language is the decision to revise the *OED* for a third edition.[20]

---

[17] A sampling reveals that they read certain works by Bale, William Barlow, and Fish. Alexander Alane's ("Alesius'") three English works, and whatever prefaces John Rogers wrote for his many editions of reform works, they excluded. They read Christopher St. German's two dialogues short-titled *Doctor and Student* in a 1638 edition which I suspect modernized the accidentals.

[18] James L. Harner, *Literary Research Guide: A Guide to Reference Sources for the Study of Literatures in English and Related Topics*, 2nd ed. (New York: MLA, 1993), 211, #1860; Angus McIntosh, M. L. Samuels, and Michael Benskin, comps., *A Linguistic Atlas of Late Mediaeval English*, 4 vols. (Aberdeen: Aberdeen Univ. Press, 1986).

[19] In 1993 Richard W. Bailey, who heads the project for an early modern English dictionary spanning 1475–1700, kindly searched MEMEM for me, for a sample of Tyndale's forms not recorded in the *OED* nor *MED*, but found no corroboration.

[20] For a representative announcement and statement of purpose, see *Scholars of Early Modern Studies* 28 (Autumn 1994): 5.

Tyndale's English need not nor cannot be explored through lexicography alone: the forces exerted by expatriation, persecution, and printing on the continent loom large. As a fugitive from the church's justice, Tyndale might have found himself forced to settle for ramshackle printing at cynically elevated prices. Instead, he achieved what looks to have been a tonic alliance with Johan Hoochstraten of Antwerp (alias "Hans Luft" of "Marlborow in the lande of Hesse" and "Adam Anonymus [sic]" of Basel).[21] As a member of what we call the "Marburg" group of books, printed by Hoochstraten for Tyndale and certain of his associates, the 1528 *Obedience* is neatly printed on high-quality (i.e., durable) paper in "Schwabacher" (or "bastard" gothic), a graceful and pleasantly legible typeface. The only appreciable cosmetic flaw is the wobbliness in the type of some of Tyndale's marginal glosses: the scabbards needed to lock these in place seem to have been in disrepair. The book contains a thirteen-item errata list drawn up by the press corrector (whose place Tyndale could have taken).[22]

---

[21] M. E. Kronenberg, "De Geheimzinnige Drukkers Adam Anonymus te Babel en Hans Luft te Marburg Ontmaskerd," *Het Boek* 8 (1919): 241–279; and "Notes on English Printing in the Low Countries (Early Sixteenth Century)," *The Library*, 4th ser., 9 (1928–1929): 139–163. See also Anne Richardson, "The Evidence against an English First Edition of Tyndale's *Obedience*," *Moreana* 13, no. 52 (November 1976): 47–52.

Here I must introduce an eleventh-hour observation that may invalidate some of the assertions about Tyndale and typesetting that follow in the body of this essay. To the best of my knowledge, it is widely believed that an early modern compositor needed enough competence in the language of the text he was setting to syllabicate properly and to vary acceptable (how so determined?) spellings, in order to achieve flush-right line justification. It seems that Tyndale / Hoochstraten dispensed with all that. The compositor of the 1528 *Obedience*, English-speaking or not, was evidently authorized to break words summarily at the penultimate position in the line, blithely tack on a hyphen and complete the word fragment in the next line. One example out of hundreds will suffice: *vnfayne-dly* (A2/6–7). Under this liberal rule, text could be set in type letter by letter, requiring of the compositor no knowledge of English. The two other works printed by Hoochstraten and known to be by Tyndale—*The Parable of the Wicked Mammon*, STC 24454, and *The Practice of Prelates*, STC 24465—follow the same compositorial pattern. Time is not available to survey the methods followed by the other printers Tyndale engaged in his lifetime. The essential question posed by any such enquiry is, I think, whether a lenient and rather mechanical policy with respect to line justification resulted in more—or less—fidelity to the English Tyndale actually wrote.

[22] Philip Gaskell, *A New Introduction to Bibliography* (Oxford: Clarendon Press, 1972), 111. I am most grateful to Katharine F. Pantzer for her helpful advice at the onset of my work on this topic.

A grim challenge to Hoochstraten's work for Tyndale was Charles V's acti-
vation of the state's punitive machinery against heresy. In 1528 there must
have been discussion of the punishments (generally, various forms of maiming
pour décourager des autres) for printers who collaborated with heretics, in what
became Charles V's 1532 criminal code, the "Carolina."[23] Perhaps, from
Tyndale's point of view, Charles's afflictive sanctions actually had the benign
effect of intimidating the less ethical printers and thus of bringing the best
people to the fore. It would be good to know more about Hoochstraten and
his kind.

A question posed by this collaboration and its products is the extent to
which the printing process—the path of Tyndale's copy from its lodging in
the visorium to its words on the page—altered what the 1528 *Obedience* said
as written. Two hypotheses, neither of which has been advanced in print, are
quick to assign responsibility to Hoochstraten's compositors for any strangeness
in Tyndale's printed expressions. I believe this judgement premature. Courting
feedback, I present the handful of spellings in the *Obedience* that I currently
regard as authorial. They are noted in the *OED* and *MED* vestigially if at all.
This category includes ubiquitous or very frequent expressions:

> *bedger* (vb.) G5v/12, *bedger* (n.) K4v/1, *bedgerd* V1/3, *bedgers* I8/25–26
> and gloss, *bedgett* A3v/14, *bedginge* K5/19,[24] *bis(s)hap(p)(e)s* A4/13,
> *sherch* B6/8, *sherched* B6/14,[25] *shercheth* F7/13, *sherchinge* (adj.) F7/21,
> *vnsherchable* S4/10–11; *this* for *thus* L2/1; and *wordly* (adj.) A7/20,
> *wordly* (adv.) G1/3—this last form is, arguably, covered in the
> *OED*.[26]

There occur also orthographic patterns, such as *e* following a long vowel or
diphthong:

---

[23] According to Jonathan Zophy in *The Holy Roman Empire: A Dictionary Handbook*
(Westbrook, CT: Greenwood Press, 1980), 391, 492, the *Constitutio criminalis Carolina*
was formulated in reaction to the Knights' War (1522–1523) and the Peasants' War
(1524–1526). This early origin suggests that its bearings were known as early as 1528.
J. F. Mozley, *William Tyndale* (London: SPCK, 1937), 124 n., refers to an edict of
October 1531 in which underground printers "might be branded with a red hot iron,
and lose an eye or a hand at the discretion of the judge."

[24] But the *OED* records *bedgarly* (s.v. *Beggarly*).

[25] The *MED* uniquely records the preterit, *sherched*.

[26] *Wordly* is handled in the present *OED* far too obscurely, as a combination of
word (a spelling of *world* contemporaneous with Tyndale) and suffix -*ly*. It naturally
gets confused with the later coinage, "wordly wise," i.e., wise in verbal constructs
only. Tyndale, however, uses *wordly* and *worldly* irrespective of that distinction.

fayeth H8v/19, *waeye* D7v/18 gloss, *wayet* (for *wait*) E6/28 gloss, and *yoeke* F6v/7.

There is a pattern of employment of *ea* for short *e*:

previleage E1/5 gloss, *purchease* F1v/16, *reamedies* S3/7 gloss, *reaported* I7v/17, and *treaspase* N7/19.

The following, too numerous to dismiss, seem to be instances of uvular and velar fricatives in *ch*, *gh* or *h*:

allehoryes R4v/30–31, *belonheth* D6v/27, *encheritaunce* G7v/8, *enhlish* C3v/30, *exceadinghly* I5/23, *lonhe* N1v/16–17, *strenghted* P5v/21.

There is a sprinkling of coinages and portmanteau words that no general dictionary should be obliged to enter:

bis(s)hap(p)(e)s (see above), *compolde* (= *compelled* + *polled*) B7/23, *disgresse* (= *degrade* from orders, = *disgrace*, = "*de-grease*" by having palms symbolically scraped to remove anointing oil) K1v/21, *divininite* (= *divinity* + *ninny*) G8v/1, *Knaveate* (Lat. vb., pl. imp.; "Play the knave") K1/25 gloss, *misshapes* (for *bishops*), P1/1, P2/1.

We conclude with isolated spellings that should be brought afresh to lexicographers' attention.

Ambasiasies V2v/7, *Emperioure* E6/11, *fanynge* C5/14 gloss, *feeders* (for *feathers*) F4v/6–7, *gyrkyn* (the incomplete *MED* will treat this form under entry-word *yarken*) I4v/28, *gysse* (for *geese*) C4/4, *hoe* (for *how*) K5v/9, *hyeres* (*heirs*) S6/13, *imagion* E5/20, *kindes* and *kyndes* (for *kindness*) E2v/31 and M2/31, *labeureth* H7/30, *lawears* K1/24, *leade* (for *laid*) H8v/29, *loost* (for *lost*) R4v/27 gloss, *overser* I7v/22, *pharesay* N2v/14, *scapfre* (immune to prosecution by adopting the tonsure, *scap* being a recorded spelling for *scalp*?) V5v/20, *seaith* N7/28, *serves* (pl., "offices") M3/4, *stocke blynde* (*stocke* for *stark*?—*OED* first records Wycherley, 1675) Q2/31, *strifte* S3v/27, *the selfe* (for *thyself*) D4v/28 gloss, *vengaunce* B3v/8, *vsary* L8/5–6, *wayx* I4/22, *whorshepe* H6/22.

The best orthographical corroboration for Tyndale's use of the forms presented here is their appearance in his other works. If one lacks convenient access to their first editions, one can mine the lists of rejected forms very properly furnished by modern editors. N. Hardy Wallis, in his 1938 edition of Tyndale's 1534 New Testament with variants from the 1525–1526 edition, exemplifies Speed Hill's rule that a critical edition of a text will "[make] it clear what is transmitted, *what suppressed*, in full detail ..." (emphasis mine).[27] Hardy Wallis's rejected "Misprints," 625–628, include *bedgerly, bedgarly, least* (for *lest*), *this* (for *thus*), *lenght, strenght* (involving fricatives), and (in 1938, innocent of the *MED's* display of the *o/a* phenomenon): *olso, ond, onother, opostle, wos* (for *was*).

With these data before us, we confront the compositorial hypotheses.

The first of these, a woolly moonbeam, holds that the compositors whimsically tampered with Tyndale's spellings in order to give them a Flemish *timbre*. Wytze Gs. Hellinga and Philip Gaskell invalidate that, citing the rule that a compositor who departed from copy had to make good his errors without pay.[28] The other hypothesis, far more plausible, explains the unusual spellings as the errors of compositors who knew too little English for their task. For this one must imagine a Flemish monoglot setting Tyndale's text letter by letter, in lexical and logical incomprehension. Solidly trained to read type in the composing stick "upside down and mirror-fashion," he would nevertheless lack a gestalt for the English words in flow, and could not spot errors that could be economically corrected in the composing stick.[29] His attempts to justify the lines by drawing on a canon of orthographic distinctions he did not possess, would be amateurish and require much resetting. Why need Hoochstraten—or Tyndale—tolerate such a bottleneck? I propose that in incurring the drastic risks of doing business with hunted expatriates, any printer Tyndale could have found would have had to focus on solvency and profit—in the shape of ready cash for getting out of the country, should that be necessary. Antwerp was the continental center for English exports and sustained a large English population. It would not have ranked as a prodigious achievement to retain one or more bilingual compositors who ably, swiftly (and expensively) prepared for print what Tyndale wrote. That there is in the 1528 *Obedience* a quantity of mechanical misprints, such as turned letters or fragments not negotiable as words (e.g., *receaveh* for *receaveth*), averaging thirty-nine instances per one hundred pages of transcription of the text, suggests that

---

[27] "The Theory and Practice of Transcription," *New Ways of Looking at Old Texts: Papers of the Renaissance English Text Society, 1985–1991,* ed. W. Speed Hill (Binghamton, NY: Medieval & Renaissance Texts & Studies, 1993), 25.

[28] Wytze Gs. Hellinga, *Copy and Print in the Netherlands . . .* , introd. H. de la Fontaine Verwey and G. W. Ovink (Amsterdam: North-Holland, 1962), 103; Gaskell, *A New Introduction,* 45, 348.

[29] Gaskell, *A New Introduction,* 45, makes the key point that correction in the composing stick could keep down costs of the press corrector's time and of elaborate corrections in proof.

Tyndale may have agreed to pass up the expensive steps of the press corrector's reading and of the resetting. Tyndale's readers could have coped with some obvious, trivial errors as long as his English had been clearly set.

There remains the question, necessary for discriminating possible compositors' errors from the authentic spellings in Tyndale's copy: how did Tyndale hear and speak the English he wrote, and what extrinsic corroboration can be advanced for this? I believe that there is, potentially, strong support in the historical/cartographic linguistics of such team efforts as the McIntosh source alluded to earlier. But dialectologists and phonologists, historical or contemporary, have their gear and tackle and trim; that is, their "mystery." And with some exceptions—Charles Barber (a grammarian, principally), E. J. Dobson, A. H. Smith, and J. C. Wells[30]—they seem unaware of what powerful applications their work could have for other disciplines such as our own. In consulting McIntosh I have been unable to get a purchase on what a "county dictionary" is, and what situation it is expected to clarify, or, if they provide dot maps to localize pronunciations, an explanation why item maps—of full words—answer a different need. Then, when a cultural historian makes the unsupported assertion that "Tyndale spoke with a plebeian, accented vernacular voice" (all his life, we are to presume[31]), one is poorly tutored for a rebuttal on dialectal or phonological grounds. Personally, I conjecture that Tyndale, beginning his long Oxford career at age eleven or twelve at the elite Magdalen School, may have suppressed his native accent and acquired what E. J. Dobson calls "standard" English, "the 'correct' speech of the educated classes" (Dobson, 1: v). Citing the work of Derek Bickerton, Wells calls this speech the "acrolect" or "the prestige norm ... associated with the highest social stratum" (Wells, 1: 18). It seems possible that the adult Tyndale had a two-tiered consciousness of his English, and that his native dialect—possibly Welsh-influenced—took over his spellings at times. Such a theory would allow us not to normalize *enhlish*, even if it occurs in close proximity to the standard form:

Hath [God] not made the *english* tonge? Why forbidde ye hym to

---

[30] Charles Barber, *Early Modern English* (London: Deutsch, 1976); E. J. Dobson, *English Pronunciation, 1500–1700*, 2 vols. (Oxford: Oxford Univ. Press, 1957); A. H. Smith, *The Place-Names of Gloucestershire*, English Place-Name Society, 4 vols. (Cambridge: Cambridge Univ. Press, 1964–1965); J. C. Wells, *Accents of English*, 3 vols. (Cambridge: Cambridge Univ. Press, 1982). I am most grateful, as well, to Anne Hudson, who in a letter to me of 4 October 1991 vetted my decisions regarding unusual spellings and made me aware of E. J. Dobson's book.

[31] David Rollison, *The Local Origins of Modern Society: Gloucestershire 1500–1800* (London: Routledge, 1992), 94.

speake in the *enhlish* tonge then / as well as in the latyne? (C3v/28–
31)

Much work from many disciplines is needed to bring Tyndale's English into
the understanding it deserves. We can be most thankful for the effort towards
a rigorous new *OED*. Its strong tide will lift Tyndale's great Admiral along
with smaller craft. Eventually, perhaps, *TLS* will run a teaser, "Has William
Tyndale been Overrated?" Then we'll know we've won!

On Editing Queen Katherine Parr

T HE BOOKMARK WITH KATHERINE PARR'S LIKENESS THAT I BOUGHT
in the shop of the National Portrait Gallery in London bore the
following brief identification:

This portrait of Catherine Parr (1512–1548), the only known likeness
of her, was painted during her four-year marriage to Henry VIII. She
nursed the ailing King as well as providing kindness to his three
children, Mary, Elizabeth and Edward. A contemporary described her
as combining "a pregnant wittiness with right wonderful grace of
eloquence". As Henry's sixth wife she out-lived him; having swiftly
re-married after his death, Catherine herself died in childbirth a year
later.[1]

---

[1] The bookmark's text should have read "the only surely authenticated likeness"
of Katherine Parr. See William A. Sessions, "The Earl of Surrey and Catherine Parr:
A Letter and Two Portraits," *American Notes and Queries,* n.s., 5.2,3 (April, July 1992):
128–130, who builds on Roy Strong's identification of the painter as William Scrots
and establishes a date for the portrait of November 1545. Among other claimed
likenessess that I have personally seen, the miniature portrait formerly known as the
Strawberry Hill miniature, now in Sudeley Castle, Gloucestershire, and the Lambeth
Palace portrait that hangs in the present archiepiscopal reception room have arguable
claims to genuineness. The portrait now at Anglesey Abbey, Cambridgeshire, which
I know only from a black-and-white photographic reproduction available from the
Courtauld Institute of Art, University of London, appears to be a copy of the Scrots
portrait.

"A pregnant wittiness with right wonderful grace of eloquence," but no word whatsoever of the evidence of these qualities that this queen put on public display in the two religious prose works that she published in her lifetime. A complete unawareness of Katherine Parr's authorship is current as well in scholarly circles. As I went about working on my edition of Parr, a library staff member at a Cambridge college reiterated an exclamation that several academics had already made to me, "But I never knew that Katherine Parr had written anything." The staff member's colleague who stood nearby added: "And published too. How did Henry ever allow one of his queens to do such a thing?"

The answer to that question, insofar as we can surmise it, is that in Henry's lifetime—that is, before late 1547—Katherine Parr got the king's permission to publish only what could be passed off as the demure enterprise of compiling a vernacular aid to personal piety. We know from several essays in the valuable collection edited by Margaret Hannay, *Silent but for the Word*,[2] that such an enterprise came just within the limits of public literary effort that could be permitted to a learned woman of royal or courtly standing by late Henrician norms. The colophon of Parr's first publication is dated 6 November 1545. Its title duly (or dutifully) highlights the contents as *Prayers or Medytacions, wherein the mynd is stirred . . . alwaie to longe for the everlastynge felicitee: Collected out of holy woorkes by the most vertuous and graciouse Princesse Katherine quene of Englande, Fraunce, and Irelande* (STC 4818).

Elsewhere I have argued that these *Prayers or Medytacions* are no mere desultory reshuffling of excerpts from book 3 of Thomas à Kempis' *De imitatio Christi* in the English translation published by Richard Whytford about 1530 (a source discovery owing to C. Fenno Hoffman, Jr.).[3] Parr's *Prayers or Medytacions* is a systematic project of reauthoring, pursued in continuous minute changes that demonasticize the *Imitatio* and open up a loving, intimate relation to Christ as the Word of Scripture for both sexes of lay Christians. The rhetorical recasting is radical, but the devotional procedures remain traditional: private saturation in the text of the Bible and meditation according to Christological patterns of interpretation. The work ends with two (later expanding to five) apparently original prayers by Parr, the first invoking God's guidance and protection for King Henry VIII, the second for men to say entering into

---

[2] *Tudor Women as Patrons, Translators, and Writers of Religious Works* (Kent, OH: Kent State Univ. Press, 1985).

[3] Janel Mueller, "Devotion as Difference: Intertextuality in Queen Katherine Parr's *Prayers or Meditations* (1545)," *Huntington Library Quarterly* 53 (1990): 171–197; C. Fenno Hoffman, Jr., "Catherine Parr as a Woman of Letters," ibid. 23 (1959): 349–397, esp. 354 n.

battle. The match between contents and immediate circumstances of publication is so clear in the *Prayers or Medytacions* that the grounds of permission becomes clear as well. Henry could not only countenance but directly authorize this timely exercise in popularizing the national religion on the part of a queen whom he trusted enough to appoint regent of the realm while he went on his last futile campaign to recapture English territories in France in 1545.[4]

Accordingly, the first seven editions of the *Prayers or Medytacions*—two in 1545, two in 1547, one in 1548, and two ca. 1550—appear from the press of the king's printer, Thomas Berthelet, and carry the stipulation "*Cum privilegio ad imprimendum solum*" in their colophons.[5] These editions are meticulously set, exhibiting such a low incidence of substantive and nonsubstantive variants, except for the constant play of spelling differences, that close inspection is required even to identify discrete editions.

The circumstances are entirely otherwise with Parr's second prose work, *The lamentacion of a sinner, made by the most vertuous Ladie, Quene Caterin, bewaylyng the ignoraunce of her blind life,* which first appeared with a colophon dated 5 November 1547, exactly two years after *Prayers or Medytacions* and, significantly, a little more that nine months after Henry's death. Sometime in the spring of 1547 Katherine Parr had precipitously and secretly married Thomas Seymour, lord admiral of the realm and the boy-king's younger uncle. These continuing connections with Edward's court were enough to secure publication of Parr's *Lamentacion* by another of the royally authorized printers, Edward Whitchurch, who brought out its first two editions in 1547 and 1548, again with the stipulation of a sole privilege to publish and again with such scrupulosity in printing that the revised STC miscategorizes the second edition of the *Lamentacion* in the holdings of Cambridge University Library as the first edition.

Nevertheless, by the late Henrician norms that applied to its date of probable composition in 1545–1546, Katherine Parr's *Lamentacion of a sinner* registers as a scandal several times compounded. It was an original exercise of author-

---

[4] These circumstances include the complementary character of Parr's *Prayers or Medytacions* and the English *Litanie* that Archbishop Cranmer prepared and Henry authorized for use at the solemn welcome given to the English troops returning from the French wars. Parr's is a handbook for private prayer in the vernacular, Cranmer's a handbook for public prayer in the vernacular. Early recognition of their complementarity is evidenced in their binding together—for example, in the Magdalene College, Cambridge, copy of the first edition of *Prayers or Medytacions* (STC 4818) and in the British Library copy of the tenth edition of 1559 (STC 4826).

[5] These are the editions designated 4818, 4818.5, 4819, 4822, 4822.5, 4823, and 4824 in Pollard and Redgrave, eds., *Short-Title Catalogue,* rev. Jackson, Ferguson, and Pantzer.

ship on the queen's part. It was a public recounting of her soul's inward struggles with severe feelings of guilt in the process of embracing justification by faith and thus proclaiming her conversion from Catholicism to an unmistakably Lutheran and hence proscribed vein of Protestantism. Most of all, this work was nothing that queen Katherine could even have imagined trying to publish after a hostile faction at court, spearheaded by Stephen Gardiner, nearly succeeded in a plot to accuse her of heresy and of both wifely and political insubordination to Henry in the spring of 1546. The very same plot brought a member of her court circle, Anne Askew, to death by burning at the stake, insuring that Askew's own written record of her first and second *Examinations* at the often illegally proceeding hands of the law would be at best a posthumous publication. These *Examinations* are the only other original work from the Henrician era, besides Parr's own, known to have been authored by an English woman.[6] So, then, signs of factual ignorance aside, the question put to me by the library staff member was at bottom a cognizant one. It accurately intuited the dangers braved by Katherine Parr as she authored and then contrived to publish her two English works under the stamp of royal privilege, all the while that the political climate about her altered completely.

It will be obvious that I have offered these opening remarks as a not very oblique rationale for the critical edition of Parr on which I am now engaged and on which I would very much welcome suggestions and comment. Let me summarize my sense of her importance as a writer of her era and then go on to address more specifically editorial considerations. First, Katherine Parr bids for attention because of her expressiveness in documenting, through her own progression from reworking an existing source to original composition, the complicated nuances of religious sensibility that characterize the first generation of those key figures with court connections who underwent the Henrician Reformation not just as a political imperative, but ultimately as a conversion experience.[7] Indeed, Parr's *Lamentacion* looks to be the earliest

---

[6] For further discussion and references, see Janel Mueller, "A Tudor Queen Finds Voice: Katherine Parr's *Lamentacion of a Sinner*," in Heather Dubrow and Richard Strier, eds., *The Historical Renaissance: New Essays on Tudor and Stuart Literature and Culture* (Chicago: Univ. of Chicago Press, 1988), 15–47, esp. 33–34.

[7] On the plane of literary composition, the conversion experience moves toward newness and rupture while always carrying a heavy residue of syncretism. Various scholars have emphasized Parr's specific indebtedness to Erasmus: see James Kelsey McConica, *English Humanists and Reformation Politics under Henry VIII and Edward VI* (Oxford: Clarendon Press, 1965), 200–234; William P. Haugaard, "Katherine Parr: The Religious Convictions of a Renaissance Queen," *Renaissance Quarterly* 22 (1979): 346–359; E. J. Devereux, "The Publication of the English Paraphrases of Erasmus,"

Protestant conversion narrative in English, the launching of a genre that would eventually become crucial in and for New England Puritanism. We lack any such conversion narrative from Tyndale, say, or Cranmer, while Latimer's sermons make only scattered half-gestures in this direction. In the second place, there is the importance and interest of women's witness in religious authorship in a newly Protestant England; as I have said, Parr is the only woman other than Askew to provide this kind of key transitional record. Third, there is the demonstrable evidence that Katherine Parr exerted a continuing influence on Elizabeth's piety.

The subject is too rich and extensive to treat adequately here, especially if I were to trace the intertextual connections with Parr's writings that I have noted in the writings of Elizabeth. Instead, in the interests of brevity, I will sketch a spectrum of rather more material linkages. The earliest is found in the princess Elizabeth's translation of Marguerite of Navarre's *Mirror of the Sinful Soul* from French into a beautiful calligraphic English as a New Year's gift for queen Katherine in 1545; here Elizabeth's covering letter submits the enterprise to her stepmother's judgment and correction while her prefatory letter "To the Reader" also marks an explicit affirmation of justification by faith to the only reader envisaged—namely, Parr.[8] As queen, the adult Elizabeth continued to venerate Katherine Parr as a model and authority for her religious guidance. The British Museum's Department of Medieval and Later Antiquities preserves an exquisite girdle prayer-book with covers wrought with biblical scenes in enamel embossed in relief, the product of a court goldsmith's art from about 1540. According to an eighteenth-century report on a now lost memorandum that had been inserted in this opulent miniature prayer-book, it was a personal possession of queen Elizabeth's. The attribution of ownership is plausible if unverifiable; what can be stated as fact is that the unknown original contents of this girdle prayer-book's ornate binding were replaced by a very tiny (32 mm x 40 mm) print of women-authored devotional materials prominently featuring Parr's *Prayers or Medytacions* and dated

Bulletin of the John Rylands Library 51 (1968–1969): 348–367, esp. 354–360; Anthony Martienssen, *Queen Katherine Parr* (London: Secker & Warburg; New York: McGraw-Hill, 1973), 1–28, 144–225; and John N. King, "Patronage and Piety: The Influence of Catherine Parr," in Hannay, ed., *Silent but for the Word,* 43–60. At the symposium "Attending to Early Modern Women," held at the University of Maryland, College Park, April 21–23, 1994, I offered evidence of her indebtedness to the work of John Fisher, Bishop of Rochester, executed with Thomas More in 1536 for refusing to swear under oath that Henry VIII was the supreme head of the church of England.

[8] Bodleian Library, Smith MS 68, Art. 50, fols. 51r–52v. See Marc Shell's transcription and annotations of Elizabeth's translation in his *Elizabeth's Glass* (Lincoln: Univ. of Nebraska Press, 1993).

1574—the only recorded exemplar of this particular edition.[9] Perhaps the most indicative material evidence of the continuities between Parr's and Elizabeth's piety is the sequencing and formatting of items in the first volume of Thomas Bentley's *The Monument of Matrones*. This is a 1582 compilation of English women's religious writings whose title page records Elizabeth's authorization to publish "*Cum privilegio Reginae Maiestatis*." Here unfold in sequence the first English printing of Elizabeth's girlish translation of the *Mirror of the Sinful Soul*, retitled *A Godlie Meditation*, directly followed by three brief English prayers by queen Elizabeth, and just as directly followed by Katherine's *Lamentacion of a sinner* and *Prayers or Medytacions*, with continuous pagination.[10]

Let me now turn, as promised, to considerations specific and pertinent to the editing of Katherine Parr. There is, first, the lack of any satisfactory modern edition of either work. As far as I know, the *Prayers or Medytacions* has not been printed since 1640. The *Lamentacion of a sinner* has seen one reprint, in *The Harleian Miscellany* for 1808 and subsequent issues.[11] However, this modern-spelling version comes unannotated and stripped of the copious marginal glosses that are an indispensable period feature of the early editions. It is of little scholarly value beyond the help it has provided to interested readers in making this text more widely accessible.

I have already alluded to some textual ramifications of the fact that Parr's two prose works appeared under royal authorization from the presses of Berthelet and Whitchurch, respectively, and were set as carefully as primers, Bibles, or the *Book of Common Prayer*. The *Lamentacion*, a text of approximately 15,000 words, shows only twelve substantive variants between its first edition of 1547 and its second of 1548, the only editions to appear in Parr's lifetime. Collation and pagination are identical in 1547 and 1548—ABCDEF$_8$G$_5$—although catchwords, spelling, punctuation, and page contents vary within these narrow confines. The 1548 edition of the *Lamentacion* offers seven substantive corrections to 1547 readings in the body of the text; to

---

[9] STC 4826.6. For further description of this superb jeweled repository for Katherine's work (shelfmark MLA 94.7–29.1), see Hugh Tait, *Seven Thousand Years of Jewellery* (London: British Museum Publications, 1986), 152; on the less than complete assurance that the girdle prayer-book was Elizabeth's, see H[ugh] T[ait's] exhibition catalogue entry, No. 11, in *Princely Magnificence: Court Jewels of the Renaissance, 1500–1603* (London: Victoria and Albert Museum, 1980). I thank John N. King for the latter reference.

[10] Thomas Bentley, *The Monument of Matrones* (London: Henry Denham, 1582) (STC 1892); I have examined the Bodleian Library's copy, shelfmark 4° C38 Jur.

[11] (London: Robert Dutton, 1808), 1: 286–313.

illustrate their nature, I simply list them. They consist of the change from "all things is all" to "all thinges in all," from "what shold I seke for refuge and comfort?" to "where shold I seke for refuge and comfort?," from "contrary" to "contrarily," from "bearing downe" to "beating downe," from "almoste great blasphemie" to "a most greate blasphemie," from "goddes wordes" to "Goddes woorde," and from "cum hedlyng" to "runne hedlyng."[12] In addition, 1548 corrects three errors in 1547's marginal headings and notes, but 1548 also introduces three new errors in numbering references and ostensibly errs further in dropping two of 1547's marginal headings in the immediate contexts of page breaks. Since I can see no grounds for ascribing such relatively minor and intermittent substantive emendations to authorial agency, and since Parr sustained her difficult, illness-ridden, and eventually fatal pregnancy from mid-January to mid-October 1548, I propose to take 1547 as my copy-text of the *Lamentacion* as being closer to Parr's own spelling and punctuation but to incorporate the corrections from 1548, appropriately recorded, of course, in the apparatus.

Excluding its brief appended prayers, which vary between two and five in number from edition to edition, the *Prayers or Medytacions* is a considerably shorter work than the *Lamentacion,* at approximately 4,500 words for the body of the text proper. Again the sustained accuracy of Berthelet's printing can be gauged from the count of substantive variants—a total of sixteen yielded by collation of the five editions that had appeared by the time of Parr's death. However, and most notably, for the first two-thirds of the *Prayers or Medytacions* there exists a holograph text in Parr's exquisite italic hand, now preserved in the Town Hall in Kendal, Cumbria. This is a tiny volume in a chased silver casing with hinged silver covers with leaves (measuring 39 mm x 52 mm) illuminated in two shades of red, two shades of blue, and gold, Queen Katherine prepared this gift at an unknown date for an otherwise unspecified Mistress Tuke, one of the three daughters of Sir Brian Tuke, a secretary to Henry VIII.

In a 1990 article, I relied on a 1980 publication by G. E. Pallant–Sidaway that represents itself as an annotated old-spelling transcription of Parr's holograph at Kendal.[13] As a result, I mistakenly described and discussed the contents of this tiny volume as comprising an entirely different ordering of a subset of material from the longer printed version of *Prayers or Medytacions.* Three years later, with the kind permission of the Kendal Town Council

---

[12] *Lamentacion of a sinner,* sigs. 9, A8r, C3r, C3v, F3r [2], F8v.

[13] *Queen Katherine Parr's Book of Prayers, Scribed, Decorated and Annotated for Kendal Parish Church* (Kendal, Cumbria, April 1980), 32 pp.

treasurer and historian, Percy Duff, I was able to examine and transcribe Parr's
Kendal holograph. As far as it goes, it is in word-for-word conformity with
the longer printed versions; the reordering in Pallant–Sidaway's booklet has no
basis whatsoever in Parr. The Kendal holograph offers valuable evidence regarding Parr's own presentation of the text in versicles, like the text of scripture, as well as her practices in word division, punctuation, and spelling.[14] I
will use the Kendal holograph as my copy-text for *Prayers or Medytacions* and
supply the remaining third of the text from the first edition of 1545, since its
readings prove correct in fifteen of the sixteen cases of substantive variants in
the early editions, the single exception being a turned letter (sig. B2r) which
results in the reading "cleane" instead of the correct "cleaue." Fortunately this
segment of text overlaps with Parr's holograph, which reads "cleaue," as do all
the other Berthelet editions.

Finding myself out of time without the opportunity to do more than state
the rationale for my edition of Katherine Parr and the considerations that have
figured in my choice of copy-texts, let me conclude by enumerating some
questions and problems that hang in the balance for me. One is the question
of editorial intervention in the matter of paragraphing. The *Prayers or Medytacions* are no problem; their versicle format means that they are paragraphed
at the end of every sentence unit. But in the sixteenth-century editions of the
Lamentacion, there is a clear dynamics of exchange to be noted. The earliest
editions have copious marginal headings and glosses but no paragraphing
policy as such; paragraphs occur if and only if the end of a sentence on a
given line does not leave room for printing the first word of the next sentence
on the same line. Then along comes Thomas Bentley's *Monument of Matrones*
(1582), which deletes all marginal headings and glosses from the *Lamentacion*
while also dividing the text into twelve titled chapters and, more locally, into
paragraph units throughout. Bentley retains the versicle format in printing the
Prayers or Medytacions while also superimposing seven titled chapters on its text.
His divisions are skillful, even sensitive, as is the wording of his chapter titles.
Queen Elizabeth authorized Bentley's edition, which contains the first English
printings of some of her own work. Can it, should it have any status in determining aspects of editorial policy in a late twentieth-century critical edition
where reception history might be expected to figure? But if so, on what
grounds? And if not, on what grounds?

Another question that nags in my mind is whether to include letters by
Katherine Parr in this edition. I have transcribed from her holographs some

---

[14] Although Tudor women, including Elizabeth, typically show a range of idiosyncratic spellings in their written English, Parr does not.

letters that I would like very much to incorporate: one in Latin to prince Edward, encouraging him with warm praise to keep writing to her in that language. The English letters include two to Henry in France that contain a mixture of political and domestic news and show Katherine in her dual roles as regent of the realm and wife to its sovereign; one to Cambridge University representatives who petitioned her to intercede for them with Henry and to whom in return she gave admonitions about the central place of Christian wisdom in all worldly learning; there are also several letters to Thomas Seymour that contain remarkable indications of his sexual magnetism for her. This is a minimal wishlist on my part.

But the list provokes further questions. Other letters survive in Katherine's hand or with her sign manual as regent that are not so immediately interesting: for example, a disposition in a land dispute, a military commission. What principles apply, especially in the situation where no scholarly biography of Katherine Parr yet exists, to guide selection for a critical edition of a historically early woman writer whose corpus remains small by any ordinary standards? Questions of annotation become more urgent with the letters, especially the ones to Henry and Seymour that are much more intelligible and dynamic in the light of their replies, which fortunately also exist. But are such letters, not by Parr, to be printed in an edition of her works? And if they are not to be printed, but hers are, how and how far should annotation proceed? I have brought us to a point of entry into the difficult problem and the absorbing challenge of working out what a policy of annotation should most usefully undertake at this late twentieth-century date, even when the readership is the one that I envisage, a university-level readership with defined interests but little or no shared grounding in Tudor history, literature, and culture. Again, my closing word is to invite and be grateful for your counsel.

On Editing Foxe's
Book of Martyrs

JOHN N. KING

S EVERAL YEARS AGO I SUGGESTED THAT THE RENAISSANCE ENG-
lish Text Society undertake preliminary discussion of the feasibility of
publishing a critical edition of John Foxe's *Acts and Monuments of the
English Martyrs*. I was not surprised when several members of the Council
greeted that suggestion with incredulity. After all, the sheer size of the work
staggers the imagination, and it exists in four substantially different editions of
ever-increasing size and complexity that the compiler produced during his
lifetime. First published in 1563, the original edition is a large folio volume of
nearly 1,800 pages. That edition contains about two million words. It underwent major revision and expansion in 1570 and in 1583 as well as minor revision in 1576. The 1583 edition contains two volumes of about two thousand folio pages in double columns. With about four million words, that text
is more than double the size of the first edition. It seems safe to say that the
"Book of Martyrs" is the largest and most complicated book to appear during
the first two or three centuries of English printing history. The fourth edition
is four times the length of the Bible. It poses editorial problems that are com-
parable to its size.

Having provided these daunting statistics, I would like to announce that
the British Academy has recently approved a proposal from David M. Loades
to prepare a critical edition of the work. The present moment provides an
appropriate occasion for us to discuss the shape that a new edition of the
"Book of Martyrs" should take. It seems to me that two major questions stand

out. Do we need a new edition of "Book of Martyrs"? If we do, what form should that edition take?

To determine whether we need a new edition, we first need to examine the present standard edition. Few libraries preserve even one of the five nineteenth-century editions that were based upon the eight-volume edition produced by Stephen R. Cattley (London, 1837–1841). The 1965 facsimile reprint of Cattley's second edition (London, 1843–1849) is the version of the work that is most readily accessible in academic libraries, but it is relatively inaccessible. Claiming to base his modernization on the 1583 edition, Cattley incorporates some but not all of the material in the 1563 edition that was revised or eliminated in later editions. He disrupts Foxe's organization by rearranging material found in his copy text. He haphazardly moves material to different places within the work, or to appendices, or to footnotes. He edits, condenses, and amends marginal glosses with extreme freedom, and often moves them into footnotes or into the text as subtitles. Latin extracts find their way into footnotes. Cattley therefore produces a composite text that reconstructs Foxe's configuration of his work.

When Cattley's first volume appeared, Samuel R. Maitland censured the editor for assuming complete discretion over whether and how to alter the text. Maitland described seemingly countless examples of textual corruption; silent emendation; faulty annotation; lexicographical misunderstanding; misunderstanding of geographical names, dates, vestments, and liturgical practices; confusion among persons and places; mistranslation of Latin; misconstrual of Latin abbreviations and contractions; and other problems.[1]

The Cattley text is an unreliable guide to bibliographical investigation of the substantial differences among the four editions overseen by Foxe because it fails to indicate the edition in which a particular document originated, whether it underwent revision, or whether it was ever eliminated from or restored to particular editions. The Victorian editor therefore denies the historicity of the "Book of Martyrs," the indeterminate state of its various texts, and their contingency of meaning as contributors to and products of highly specific political, social, and cultural circumstances.

David Loades concurs with Cattley's belief that the 1576 and 1583 editions are substantially the same as that of 1570,[2] but Thomas Freeman adds that some "material added to the 1570 and 1576 editions but not included in the

---

[1] Samuel R. Maitland, *Six Letters on Fox's "Acts and Monuments," Addressed to the Editor of the "British Magazine" and Re-Printed from that Work with Notes and Additions* (London: Rivington, 1837), *passim*.

[2] David M. Loades, "A New Edition of The Acts and Monuments of the English Martyrs by John Foxe" (unpublished document).

1583 edition was completely lost" from the Victorian edition. He cites the example of Edward Alin and his wife, whose escape from captivity receives no mention in the Victorian edition because Foxe cited that incident only in the 1570 and 1576 editions.[3] We may note an example of how Foxe revises his text and how Cattley alters it and eradicates differences that exist among different editions by examining an extract from the account of George Marsh as we find it in the 1563, 1583, and 1849 editions. As Warren Wooden notes, Foxe's 1563 version contains a high degree of circumstantial detail that contributes to a portrait of the Bishop of Chester as a persecuting prelate who dies of venereal disease because of his predilection for "whorehunting." Although Foxe qualifies his attack and sacrifices circumstantial detail and rhetorical vigor in the 1583 version, the cleric's deficiencies and the cause of his death remain clear. By contrast Cattley introduces alterations for stylistic effect and bowdlerizes his modernized version of the 1583 text by referring to rumors about a "disgraceful disease" instead of the illness of a cleric who "was burneth of an harlot."[4] Bowdlerization of that kind is pervasive in the Victorian edition.[5]

The Cattley edition furthermore eradicates evidence concerning the book-making art that went into the early editions of the "Book of Martyrs." We should remember that Foxe collaborated closely with his publisher, John Day, who produced what are arguably the best Elizabethan examples of compositorial craft and woodcut illustration. The first edition of the "Book of Martyrs" contains fifty-three woodcuts, almost all of which are tailor-made to illustrate Foxe's martyrologies. Fifty-five cuts are added and only four dropped in the 1570 edition, for a total of 104 illustrations. The 1576 and 1583 editions respectively contain 104 and 103 woodcuts, of which only two represent

---

[3] Thomas Freeman, personal communication, November 29, 1992. All editions of *Acts and Monuments* are hereafter cited in the notes as *A&M*.

[4] Warren Wooden cites parallel texts in the Appendix of *John Foxe* (Boston: Twayne Publishers, 1983), 117–119.

[5] For example, Foxe reports that in 1558 Parisian clerics denounced a Huguenot congregation, "persuading the people most falsely, that they assembled together, to make a bancket in the night, and there puttyng out the candles, they went together, Jacke with Jylle (as they sayd) after a filthy and beastly manner" (*A&M* [1570], 1049). According to the Cattley edition, the clergy persuaded the people that the Protestants "assembled together to make a banquet in the night, and there, putting out the candles, they intended to commit moost filthy abominations" (*A&M* [1877]: 4: 424). The modern edition eliminates use of colloquial idiom to satirize the Catholic clergy. I am indebted to Thomas Freeman for this example.

wholly new work.[6] Foxe and/or Day integrated these illustrations carefully into the body of the work by means of textual references, commentary, and annotation. By contrast, the Cattley version contains pallidly attenuated Victorian copies of the famous title page and only twenty-seven of the woodcuts that appeared in the early editions.

By now you may have guessed my answer to the first question that I have posed. I believe that a critical edition of the "Book of Martyrs" is a major desideratum. My examination of the Cattley edition enumerates many problems that modern editors would be well advised to avoid. Let me turn to my second question: What form should a new edition take?

A consensus exists among specialists in early modern history that a critical edition should be based upon collation of the four editions that Foxe revised. Taking the 1583 edition as his copy text, David Loades would incorporate the results of collation of the other English versions overseen by Foxe into a modernized edition. He also plans to transcribe the two Latin precursors of the "Book of Martyrs."[7] To these materials he would add the biography of Foxe that first appeared in the 1641 edition. The edition would contain reproductions of all the woodcuts and a full critical apparatus. It seems likely that the Foxe project will pose editorial problems that are at least as complicated as those faced by the twentieth-century editors of the works of Thomas More, William Tyndale, and Richard Hooker. If suitable technology for computerized scanning of texts exists, it might ease some editorial difficulties. It would be best if the editorial team that undertakes this project included specialists in the history and literature of early modern Britain as well as experts in patristic studies, Byzantine studies, medieval Latin, and neo-Latin.

Patrick Collinson has issued the caveat that it would be inappropriate simply to rely upon the last edition produced during Foxe's lifetime. In each revision Foxe eliminated material "in order to accommodate more recent and exciting accessions to his knowledge." Furthermore, the compiler's manuscript papers contain narratives and source material that even he chose to exclude from his encyclopedic history. Collinson concludes that

> a basic necessity for Foxeian studies would be a critical edition of *Acts and Monuments* which at the very least would indicate the point of entry, or of departure, of every episode, passage or document, with

---

[6] Ruth Samson Luborsky and Elizabeth Morley Ingram, *A Guide to English Illustrated Books 1536–1603* (Tempe, AZ: Medieval & Renaissance Texts & Studies, 1998).

[7] John Foxe, *Commentarii rerum in ecclesia gestarum* (Strasbourg: Wendelinus Rihelius, 1554); *Rerum in Ecclesia gestarum* (Basel: Joannes Oporinus, 1559).

source references and cross references to the unpublished material in the author's papers.

He cites the example of Christopher Wade, whose extremely vivid narrative first appeared in the 1583 edition. Only on the basis of collation of the third and fourth edition can we determine why the sources for this story, Richard Fletcher, the Elder and Younger, finally provided it to Foxe a full generation after Wade's death.[8] Another good example may be found in Hugh Latimer's words of consolation to his companion, Nicholas Ridley, in what may be Foxe's best known martyrdom. According to the 1570 edition, Latimer states: "Be of good comfort, Master Ridley, and play the man. We shall this day light such a candle by God's grace in England, as I trust shall never be put out. ...." That famous sentence appears nowhere in the 1563 account of the deaths of Latimer and Ridley. It would be of genuine critical and historiographical interest to determine whether those words and others are based upon documentary records or are fictional additions by the compiler.

How would a new edition incorporate the results of collation? Because Foxe himself never stabilized his text during a lifelong process of revision, I believe it would be inappropriate to imitate Cattley by attempting to stabilize it now. The shape of the early editions might best be preserved if a transcript of the 1583 edition were prepared. Three separate—and voluminous—appendices could contain transcriptions of material absent from the 1583 edition that appeared in 1563, 1570, and 1576. An elaborate critical apparatus would be required to indicate the textual history of individual documents and narratives in line with Collinson's concerns.

What other elements should go into a new edition? As David Loades proposes, it should include facsimiles of the original illustrations. The commentary could indicate how woodcuts were added or deleted in successive volumes, how the placement of some of them changed as Foxe revised the "Book of Martyrs," and how different texts were set into empty banderoles within woodcuts. Marginalia should remain in the margins; annotation could indicate significant variation in glosses of different editions.

Every effort should be made to approximate textually significant layout and typography in the early editions. Those elements highlight the status of the "Book of Martyrs" as a compilation of documents by a variety of different hands. They therefore throw light on questions concerning Foxe's veracity, which dominated much early criticism. An ideal edition would approximate

---

[8] Patrick Collinson, "Truth and Legend: The Veracity of John Foxe's Book of Martyrs," in *Clio's Mirror: Historiography in Britain and the Netherlands,* ed. A. C. Duke and C. A. Tamse (Zutphen, Netherlands: De Walburg Pers, 1985), 36–37.

the typographical signs "that is, the shifts among different type sizes, black letter, and roman and italic fonts that differentiate Foxe's commentary from primary documents. Although the specific type fonts and sizes vary in the early editions, alternation among different fonts and sizes is both consistent and textually meaningful. I do not mean to suggest that black letter must be used, but typographical distinctions among different kinds of texts should be preserved. In the early editions, consistent usage of black letter and roman type differentiates received documents from Foxe's editorial commentary or narrative. Glosses appear in roman type and italics. Collinson notes, furthermore, that even changes in running headlines and paragraphing are textually significant. Foxe's narrative concerning Elizabeth when she was a princess, for example, was originally printed in the form of extremely long paragraphs that fail to differentiate between narrative and dialogue. Paragraphing becomes shorter and shorter in successive editions until individual speeches appear in separate paragraphs that begin to approximate dramatic representation of the kind that we encounter in Jacobean plays based upon the collection. At the same time, Foxe and/or his publisher rewrites the running headlines in order to enhance the providential aspect of the princess's experience."[9]

What kind of apparatus should a new edition contain? It would be a mistake if it failed to address the interests of specialists in both the literature and the social, political, and ecclesiastical history of early modern Britain as well as the needs of students and generally educated readers. I am afraid that an adequate commentary would have to be quite lengthy in order to identify citations, sources, historical personages, influences, places, dates, literary genres, typological constructions of characters and events, and other more or less factual information. An extended textual commentary would be required to address the issues outlined earlier in this paper. Annotation should include translations of passages in Latin and other languages. Thomas Freeman notes, furthermore, that a new edition "would make an important contribution to research on Foxe if it did nothing else but provide a good index."[10] Indices in the nineteenth-century editions are haphazard at best and inferior to those found in the sixteenth-century editions. At the present moment readers encounter considerable difficulty in locating specific materials in the "Book of Martyrs."

In conclusion, let me mention that I have not addressed the qualitative question of whether the "Book of Martyrs" warrants this kind of attention. I simply assume that it was a defining text of its age, a literary and historical

---

[9] Personal communication, December 2, 1993.

[10] Personal communication, cited above, note 3.

monument that served the nationalistic interests of the Elizabethan regime. Many of us recall the familiar story of how chained copies of this massive work were placed alongside Bibles for the edification of the people in cathedral churches throughout the realm. I have also failed to address many issues concerning the practicality of the proposed scheme for a new edition. It does seem certain, however, that the project will encounter difficulties that transcend those that we currently anticipate. Nevertheless, it is my hope that a new critical edition of Foxe's *Acts and Monuments* will eventually see the light of day despite the exigencies of modern editing and publishing that will inevitably impede the progress of this project.

Editing Romeo and Juliet: *"A challenge[,] on my life"*

JILL L. LEVENSON

O VER THE PAST DECADE OR SO, CONTINENTAL THEORY HAS infiltrated textual criticism in more than one way. Bibliographers use its vocabulary: concepts such as "foul papers" and "copy-text" have suddenly entered "the sphere of desire."[1] Outside that sphere, such concepts occupy a zone where they may be diminished or effaced. The author, expiring like a diva since the 1950s, casts only a shadow of his or her former authority. The individual text has become suspect, an inadequate representation of the processes which create a literary work. As D. C. Greetham writes on the status of evidence, "[t]he relations between substance and accidence, whole and part, truth and accuracy, cause and effect have been called into question with renewed urgency by the postmodernist dispersal of form, authority, and essentialism."[2] Narratives of all kinds—from the textual fictions which rationalize editorial biases to the "master" narratives which rationalize intellectual discipline and evidence—are breaking down under the pressure of

---

[1] This phrase comes from Jonathan Goldberg, " 'What? in a names that which we call a Rose,' The Desired Texts of *Romeo and Juliet*," in *Crisis in Editing: Texts of the English Renaissance*, ed. Randall M Leod (New York: AMS Press, Inc., 1994), 181. Goldberg connects it with "certain post-Freudian accounts."

[2] "Textual Forensics," *PMLA* 111 (1996): 47.

close examination.[3] In this space the editor, as W. Speed Hill describes the function, is demoted, diminished, decentered, and deconstructed.[4] Amid the detritus, the editing project would seem to have reached endgame: "Finished, it's finished, nearly finished, it must be nearly finished."

Yet the editing project goes on. For Shakespeare texts it flourishes: The Arden Shakespeare, The New Cambridge Shakespeare, The New Folger Library Shakespeare, A New Variorum Edition, and The Oxford Shakespeare are prominent series reissuing the plays and verse; new collected editions, such as the Norton, are appearing one after the other. Among the editors, a number are adapting or replacing the New Bibliographic model in order to present the text as multiple, dynamic, "a 'field' of force."[5] But there are limits. Publishers still treat editions as if they were "stable, achievable, objective, tangible substances . . .";[6] that is, publishers are still concerned with the bottom line, and the newer models, such as multiple texts, tend to produce more expensive editions. Publishers have a point: the academy needs affordable texts to read and to teach; the nonacademic reader needs affordable and comprehensible texts to satisfy the interest sparked by a theatrical production, a film, a public lecture, or some form of review. The introduction of hypertext or Michael Warren's infinitive format might eliminate the strain Leah S. Marcus describes "between the acknowledgment of variability and the desire to reconstruct a reliable authorial text" (54). But for the time being these formulations will not displace the printed edition for classroom use or pleasure reading; and most printed editions will continue to be governed by editorial procedures which a publisher has approved.

When I began to edit *Romeo and Juliet* for Oxford in the late 1980s, I followed a set of instructions prepared in 1978. They directed editors to what had become an uncomfortable site between textual theory and the marketplace:

> The Oxford Shakespeare will present texts newly edited in the light
> of current scholarship. . . . We hope to provide . . . volumes which

---

[3] For a definition of textual fictions, see Thomas L. Berger's review of The Oxford Shakespeare, *Analytical & Enumerative Bibliography* n.s. 3 (1989): 161; on "master" narratives, see Greetham, 32–33.

[4] See "Where We Are and How We Got There: Editing after Poststructuralism," *Shakespeare Studies* 24 (1996): 38–46.

[5] Leah S. Marcus uses this Barthean phrase in "Renaissance / Early Modern Studies," in *Redrawing the Boundaries: The Transformation of English and American Literary Studies*, ed. Stephen Greenblatt and Giles Gunn (New York: MLA, 1992), 51.

[6] Peter L. Shillingsburg, "Text as Matter, Concept, and Action," *Studies in Bibliography* 44 (1991): 38.

will be economically within the reach of students and scholars, and which will be encompassable by the mind. ... We hope to benefit from our predecessors while re-examining the conventions in the interests of providing the reader with the help he needs to read the plays with an understanding of their texts and contexts. In particular, we hope to find better ways of presenting to the reader works designed for performance.[7]

With the prospective audience in mind, I started to reexamine original documents in order to rethink the play's textual history. At the same time, I brought myself up to date on textual theory. Each reading corroborated the other: textual narrative and textual evidence did not match; current theory questioned accepted paradigms and offered a lexicon for doubt.

There are two substantive texts of *Romeo and Juliet*: the first quarto (Q1), printed in 1597 by John Danter and Edward Allde; and the second quarto (Q2), printed in 1599 by Thomas Creede for Cuthbert Burby. A third quarto (Q3), dated 1609, reprints Q2; a fourth, dated 1622 by George Walton Williams,[8] reprints Q3 with occasional consultation of Q1; the Folio reproduces an annotated copy of Q3;[9] and a fifth quarto, dated 1647, reprints the fourth. By the 1980s conjectures about the substantive versions formed a received narrative about the textual history of *Romeo and Juliet*, and the three important editions published between 1980 and 1986 repeated both its sequence and its style.[10] The narrative relates the fortunes of three texts: a "bad" quarto, a "good" quarto, and the original of both. Of course this account resembles several others contemporary with it, generated by the New Bibliography and dealing with multiple-text English Renaissance plays. It uses the idiom of Alfred W. Pollard, who first categorized Shakespeare's quartos as "good" and "bad," and who identified the first quarto of *Romeo and Juliet* as bad because

---

[7] "Editorial Procedures" (1978), 4–5. The revised "Editorial Procedures" (1991), page 7, makes virtually the same points.

[8] "The Printer and the Date of *Romeo and Juliet* Q4," *Studies in Bibliography* 18 (1965): 253–254.

[9] See S. W. Reid, "The Editing of Folio *Romeo and Juliet*," *Studies in Bibliography* 35 (1982): 43–66.

[10] In chronological order, these editions are The Arden Shakespeare, edited by Brian Gibbons (London and New York: Methuen, 1980); The New Cambridge Shakespeare, edited by G. Blakemore Evans (Cambridge: Cambridge Univ. Press, 1984); and The Oxford Shakespeare, edited by John Jowett (as part of *Shakespeare: The Complete Works*, ed. Stanley Wells and Gary Taylor [Oxford: Clarendon Press, 1986]).

it had no entry in the Stationers' Register and disagreed with the Folio text. More than once he called Q1 a "piracy," surreptitiously published.[11]

This narrative began to take shape about fifty years ago. In 1948 Harry R. Hoppe determined the fate of the 1597 quarto with the title of his monograph *The Bad Quarto of "Romeo and Juliet": A Bibliographical and Textual Study*.[12] After analyzing the printing history of Q1, he presented circumstantial evidence of memorial reconstruction by two disaffected actors, probably Romeo and Paris. During the 1940s and 1950s, W. W. Greg endorsed the legitimacy of the 1599 quarto, giving his distinguished imprimatur to a view first advanced in 1879. He claimed that most of Q2 derived from Shakespeare's holograph, only one reprinted passage and occasional bits from Q1.[13] Once the substantive texts had been characterized, scholars who followed Hoppe and Greg concentrated on figuring out the relationship of the quartos as well as their common original. John Jowett's Lachmannian genealogy in *A Textual Companion* to The Oxford Shakespeare illustrates the trend.[14]

Evidence for these speculations is scarce. It consists of three disparate kinds of facts: the dates on the title pages which indicate that Q2 was printed after Q1; differences between the two texts in length and expression; and one long segment, as well as a number of short ones, virtually identical in composition. Specifically, the first quarto is close to seventy-nine percent as long as the second (2,364 lines compared with just over 3,000 lines[15]); it contains over 800 lines which are in some ways variants of corresponding lines in the longer quarto (see Hoppe, 181–184, 189–190); and it includes several passages which

---

[11] *Shakespeare's Folios and Quartos: A Study in the Bibliography of Shakespeare's Plays 1594–1685* (London: Methuen, 1909), 65, 69. The notion of clandestine publishing derives, of course, from Heminge and Condell's address in the Folio "*To the great Variety of Readers,*" where they say that they have replaced "diverſe ſtolne, and ſurreptitious copies, maimed, and deformed by the frauds and ſtealthes of iniurious impoſtors."

[12] Cornell Studies in English, 36 (Ithaca, NY: Cornell University Press).

[13] See Greg's *The Editorial Problem in Shakespeare: A Survey of the Foundations of the Text* (Oxford: Clarendon Press, 1942), 61–62, and *The Shakespeare First Folio: Its Bibliographical and Textual History* (Oxford: Clarendon Press, 1955), 229–231. For the original version, see Robert Gericke, "Romeo and Juliet nach Shakespeare's Manuscript," *Shakespeare Jahrbuch* 14 (1879): 207–273.

[14] Ed. Stanley Wells and Gary Taylor with John Jowett and William Montgomery (Oxford: Clarendon Press, 1987), 288.

[15] The Q1 count is Barry Gaines's for The Malone Society edition currently in preparation; the Q2 count is mine.

differ completely from their equivalents.[16] Yet Q1 served as copy for Q2 at least once, for a passage of more than eighty lines;[17] Q2 follows this Q1 passage in wording, capitals, punctuation, spelling, and typography—in particular the odd use of italics for the speeches of the Nurse. It appears that the Q2 printers consulted Q1 elsewhere as well.[18] As a result, bibliographers generally agree that the first quarto has influenced the second to an extent which cannot be measured with accuracy.

This indeterminate relationship has nevertheless produced the modern orthodoxy: memorial reconstruction, a concept of transmission that has received wide acceptance since Hoppe's book made its case.[19] The theory holds that an actor or actors reproduced the play from memory either for production (possibly by Pembroke's company or in provincial tour) or for publication as Q1. The original, a form of *Romeo and Juliet* represented by Q2, may have been a variant abridged and otherwise adapted for provincial performance by Shakespeare's company; the official acting version; or both shortened and full-length renderings in combination. The actor(s) would have remembered this original from taking part in performance or reading the copy. Memory, perhaps assisted by actors' parts or bits of manuscript, may have faltered, a lapse explaining the shortness of the text. For most proponents of this theory, other failures account for other differences between Q1 and Q2. Such critics evaluate the quality of reporting by the coincidence of the two texts, and they often nominate reporters who might have produced the largest number of matching lines.

The articulation of this concept in Pollard's terms discredits the first quarto; yet Pollard's explanations collapse for lack of evidence, and the modern orthodoxy raises many questions, especially when it assumes its judgmental

---

[16] For example, 2.6; 3.2.57–60; 4.5.43–70; 5.3.13–17; act, scene, and line numbers for *Romeo and Juliet* come from *The Riverside Shakespeare*, ed. G. Blakemore Evans et al., 2nd ed. (Boston and New York: Houghton Mifflin, 1997), 1104–1145.

[17] There is some disagreement about the exact limits of the passage, which may be impossible to fix. I follow George Walton Williams, whose critical edition sets them as 1.2.53B–1.3.34 (*The Most Excellent and Lamentable Tragedie of Romeo and Juliet* [Durham, NC: Duke Univ. Press, 1964], 105).

[18] For instance, 2.1.13; 2.4.101–103; 3.5.27–31. See Gibbons's edition, 21–23, for an overview of scholarship on these bibliographical links.

[19] Tycho Mommsen first published his version of the theory in " 'Hamlet,' 1603; and 'Romeo and Juliet,' 1597," *The Athenaeum* 29 (1857): 182; Kathleen O. Irace recently endorsed it in *Reforming the "Bad" Quartos: Performance and Provenance of Six Shakespearean First Editions* (Newark, DE, London, and Toronto: Univ. of Delaware Press and Associated Univ. Presses, 1994), *passim*. My synopsis of the concept and its application to *Romeo and Juliet* is based on a body of scholarship that spans 140 years.

mode. In the first instance, non-entrance of Q1 in the Stationers' Register constitutes negative evidence: it says nothing about copyright or the way Danter acquired this version of the tragedy.[20] Moreover, differences between Q1 and the Folio have no immediate bearing on the publication of the earlier play; they may provide a basis for appraising the two extant forms of *Romeo and Juliet*, but they furnish no evidence at all about the ownership of Q1.[21]

In the second instance, no contemporary evidence survives to verify that any actor(s) ever reconstructed a play memorially; and it seems unlikely that reporters would have forgotten their own lines and cues.[22] More to the point, certain assumptions raise doubts about the logic of this theory. Advocates of memorial reconstruction generally consider the play in question corrupt, its state a sign of an illegitimate and therefore pirated manuscript. They presume that a stationer would have bought such a play and that a printer would have manufactured it as a book; they take for granted that such a procedure would have continued over many years, allowed by the companies and ignored by other publishers.[23] But no evidence confirms that any play was ever stolen from Shakespeare's company. Further, not only the actor(s) but also the stationer and printer would have taken a big risk for a small re-

---

[20] The connection between entrance in the Stationers' Register and copyright is discussed by Leo Kirschbaum, *Shakespeare and the Stationers* (Columbus: Ohio State Univ. Press, 1955), 89–91, and by S. Schoenbaum, *William Shakespeare: Records and Images* (London and New York: Scolar Press and Oxford Univ. Press, 1981), 205. Maureen Bell gives the latest statistics for "Entrance in the Stationers' Register," *The Library* 6th ser. 16 (1994): 50–54.

[21] It is worth noting that the distinction between "good" and "bad" has given an inaccurate impression of the quality of printing for the two quartos. In fact, the mistakes in Q1 are unremarkable in kind and number, fewer than in Q2.

[22] The contesting views represented in this paragraph come from Robert E. Burkhart, *Shakespeare's Bad Quartos: Deliberate Abridgments Designed for Performance by a Reduced Cast* (The Hague and Paris: Mouton, 1975), 19–22; Paul Werstine, "Narratives about Printed Shakespeare Texts: 'Foul Papers' and 'Bad Quartos,'" *Shakespeare Quarterly* 41 (1990): 65–86; David Bradley, *From Text to Performance in the Elizabethan Theatre: Preparing the Play for the Stage* (Cambridge: Cambridge Univ. Press, 1992), 9–11; Jay L. Halio, "Handy-Dandy: Q1/Q2 *Romeo and Juliet*," in *Shakespeare's "Romeo and Juliet": Texts, Contexts, and Interpretation*, ed. Jay L. Halio (Newark, DE, and London: Univ. of Delaware Press and Associated Univ. Presses, 1995), 123–150; and David Farley–Hills, "The 'Bad' Quarto of *Romeo and Juliet*," *Shakespeare Survey* 49 (1996): 27–44.

[23] According to Gary Taylor's Introduction to *A Textual Companion*, 26, during Shakespeare's lifetime playtexts different from those now considered authoritative were not published after 1609.

turn, because playbooks did not earn high profits under the most legitimate of circumstances.[24]

Fourteen years after Pollard made the distinction between good and bad quartos, Greg indicated the awkwardness with which it fit the two substantive texts of Shakespeare's early tragedy: "*Romeo and Juliet* is remarkable in that the bad text seems a good deal better, and the good text a good deal worse, than we are accustomed to find."[25] The relationship between the quartos is unusually puzzling because Q1 has theatrical associations which Q2 appears not to share. As a result, the bibliographical connection is complicated not only by the processes of writing, publication, and perhaps memory, but also by theatrical interventions of various kinds. As Paul Werstine has concluded, the early theatrical history of *Romeo and Juliet* may be embedded in the first quarto: "Yet it seems quite optimistic to believe that such raw stuff as this quarto ... will readily yield up to rational analysis the record of theatrical process it contains."[26] It is just as unlikely that Q1 will ever give an unambiguous account of the play's early textual career.

And there's the rub. Without being able to establish the copy for Q1 or the connection between the substantive texts, it is impossible to begin a stemma. For this reason, the received narrative of *Romeo and Juliet* started to come apart in the early 1980s with reviews by some of the "new revisionists"[27] of the Arden edition. For example, my colleague Randall McLeod (writing as Random Cloud) disconnected the sequence quarto by quarto:

> At odds with the judgment of the First Quarto as Bad is the repeated acknowledgment in the pages of textual introduction that Q1 is a substantive edition. ... There is another substantive edition, however, Q2 the Good, which the editor adopts for his copy-text. ... His formulation ... ignores or forgets that whatever the truth about reports and production behind Q1, there must have been a manuscript that initiated it all, and that this manuscript must bear some relation—of identity or difference—to the manuscript that underlies most of

---

[24] See Peter W. M. Blayney, "The Publication of Playbooks," in *A New History of Early English Drama*, ed. John D. Cox and David Scott Kastan (New York: Columbia Univ. Press, 1996), 383–422.

[25] "Principles of Emendation in Shakespeare," in *Aspects of Shakespeare: Being British Academy Lectures* (Oxford: Clarendon Press, 1933), 147.

[26] "The First Quarto of *Romeo and Juliet* and the Limits of Authority," typescript of a paper delivered at the 1985 meeting in New York City of the Society for Textual Scholarship, 10–11.

[27] I have adapted the phrase "new revisionists" from D. C. Greetham's *Textual Scholarship: An Introduction* (New York and London: Garland Publishing, 1992), 353.

Q2. The editor implies that they are identical. But will he state it, and can he prove it?

McLeod proposed a new formulation: the two substantive quartos witness the multiplicity of what Shakespeare wrote; the playwright may have created *Romeo and Juliet* over time and through different phases, "perhaps in several different manuscripts, each perhaps with its own characteristic aesthetic, offering together several finalities."[28]

By 1988 Jonathan Goldberg extended his own review of the Arden *Romeo and Juliet* in a paper that began with Fredson Bowers and ended with Jacques Derrida. Whatever their provenance, he argued, both substantive quartos vest their authority in theatrical performances. This fact considered, what is the relationship of the two witnesses? "Q2 is a different version—or, rather, different versions—of the play. It is a selection from or an anthology of a number of productions of *Romeo and Juliets*, one of which was close to the performance represented by Q1. . . ." And the play itself remains, in Goldberg's translation of Derrida, a "still living palimpsest."[29]

This theoretics returns my account to its point of departure. As the 1980s ended, a new skepticism was both established and, as Marcus said, "exhilarating and indispensable" for a number of critics interpreting early modern texts (51), especially plays. Warren had written his seminal essay on the two versions of Marlowe's *Doctor Faustus*; and, with Gary Taylor and Steven Urkowitz, he had challenged orthodox thinking about Quarto and Folio *King Lear*. Werstine had begun to publish a series of essays debating not only the narratives but the lexicon of the New Bibliography.[30] At the time when I needed to choose a control-text,[31] textual narratives were in various states of

---

[28] "The Marriage of Good and Bad Quartos," *Shakespeare Quarterly* 33 (1982): 423, 429.

[29] Goldberg's review appears in *Shakespeare Studies* 16 (1983): 343–348; his paper, delivered at the twenty-fourth annual Conference on Editorial Problems, University of Toronto, 4–5 November 1988, has now been published in the proceedings (see n. 1 for a complete reference), 173–201. I have taken the quotations from pages 186 and 191.

[30] For a summary of the debate over *King Lear*, see Marcus, 52–53, 63. Warren's article on Marlowe, "*Doctor Faustus*: The Old Man and the Text," appeared in *English Literary Renaissance* 11 (1981): 111–147. Werstine's essays include "The Textual Mystery of *Hamlet*," *Shakespeare Quarterly* 39 (1988): 1–26; " 'Foul Papers' and 'Prompt-Books': Printer's Copy for Shakespeare's *Comedy of Errors*," *Studies in Bibliography* 41 (1988): 232–246; and later, the article cited in n. 22 above.

[31] "Control-text" is Stanley Wells' term, defined in both the 1978 and 1991 versions of "Editorial Procedures" for The Oxford Shakespeare.

deconstruction, and I could be identified as one of those editors described by Speed Hill.

Nevertheless, certain editorial decisions seemed inevitable. I concluded that the substantive texts of *Romeo and Juliet* represent two different and legitimate kinds of witnesses to two different stages of an ongoing theatrical event. In Q2, duplication of several passages indicates authorial revision and therefore authorial working papers rather than a manuscript used in the theatre.[32] On the other hand, Q1 shows clear signs of connection with performance. Descriptive stage directions record stage business; reduced poetry and rhetoric accelerate the action; abbreviation results in a quickly paced, popular version of the play for a provincial tour or in London. Recently a few scholars have argued that Q1 is a deliberate abridgment of Q2 for performance, made by a redactor or Shakespeare himself from a holograph basically the same as the copy for Q2.[33] Peter W. M. Blayney suggests another kind of theatrical link after reviewing Humphrey Moseley's address to readers of the Beaumont and Fletcher Folio (1647). Apparently actors made copies of plays for their friends from versions usually abridged for performance, writing down what had been spoken on stage; the quality of such texts would vary according to the actors' source and procedures.[34]

How could a book display both versions, the only original inscriptions from the "still living palimpsest"? The Oxford edition will try to meet the demands of textual theory and the marketplace by treating the quartos as two versions of the play, distinct conceptions of the work at distinct points of utterance,[35] and by giving readers both for the price of one. With the agreement of Stanley Wells, the General Editor, and Oxford University Press, this

---

[32] Evidence of revision, authorial first and second thoughts preserved in the printed text, argue that Q2 came from Shakespeare's own manuscript draft. Although there is now consensus among editors and other bibliographers about the copy for Q2, there had been a debate which grew increasingly elaborate until the 1950s. Gericke originated the theory that the printers of Q2 depended on Shakespeare's manuscript but consulted Q1; G. Hjort first contended the opposite, that Q2 was printed from Q1 collated with a manuscript, in "The Good and Bad Quartos of 'Romeo and Juliet' and 'Love's Labour's Lost,'" *Modern Language Review* 21 (1926): 140–146.

[33] The most extensive studies of this kind are by Burkhart (in his chapter on *Romeo and Juliet*, 55–67), Halio, and Farley–Hills.

[34] Blayney, 393–394. A third theory about the relationship of the quartos, supported by a small but growing number of scholars since the 1980s, considers Q1 a first draft for Q2. Hoppe, 58–64, gives a history of the concept to 1948; Irace, 95–114, devotes a chapter to the general topic of revision and the return to this hypothesis in recent years by scholars such as Steven Urkowitz.

[35] The appositive paraphrases Shillingsburg's definition of a "version," 51.

edition will include Q1 as well as Q2 in modern spelling. Q2 will take its
traditional position at the front of the volume with collation and commentary;
it offers the fuller version reprinted by Shakespeare's company. Q1 will appear
without apparatus. Although I have reduced potentially confusing duplications
in Q2 (like the "dawn speech" assigned to both Romeo and Friar Laurence
in the second act), I have otherwise interfered as little as possible with either
text.[36] But I have not pursued authorial intent. I leave pursuit of all intents
to the reader, who is equipped by the commentary with detailed notes on
text, language, rhetorical devices, and staging cues. The texts themselves furnish material evidence for speculations about the relationship between the versions. In addition, I have collected profiles of 170 or so prompt books, beginning with those listed by Charles H. Shattuck,[37] recording their cuts and
stage directions. These have been entered on a data base with a World Wide
Web site that will make them available to anyone who uses my edition, or
any other, of *Romeo and Juliet*. With its information about particular lines and
stage effects, the data base becomes another means for encountering the kind
of indeterminacy which characterizes a successful play. Anyone interested can
explore the text—speech and action—through its permutations from the seventeenth to the late twentieth century. Through one book and free technology, a reader will be able to engage with as many versions of *Romeo and Juliet*
as he or she desires.

---

[36] Despite the distinction they make between the two quartos—bad and good, illegitimate and legitimate—most recent editors incorporate stage directions and readings
from Q1 into Q2, which they choose as copy-text. Evans's "Textual Analysis," 211–
212, is representative.

[37] *Shakespeare Promptbooks: A Descriptive Catalogue* (Urbana and London: Univ. of
Illinois Press, 1965), 411–432.

"Is it upon record?":
The Reduction of the History Play
To History

PAUL WERSTINE

IN SHAKESPEARE'S *RICHARD III*, AS PRINCE EDWARD IS ENTERING London, Buckingham has just affirmed to him that Julius Caesar began construction of the Tower of London. The Prince replies: "Is it upon record, or else reported / Successively from age to age, he built it?" (3.1.73–74).[1] I quote this question in full in order to call attention to the variety of what constituted histories in the early modern period. History is written record, and it is also oral report, that is, what is "reported / Successively from age to age." According to the next speech given the Prince, there is not even a hierarchy to these possible sources of history: "But say ... it were not registered, / Methinks the truth should live from age to age, / As 'twere retailed to all posterity, / Even to the general all-ending day" (76–79). As Annabel Patterson has recently reminded us in her *Reading Holinshed's Chronicles*, early modern printed histories adopted analogously inclusive protocols. Printed history was not only, to quote Patterson, "the grand-scale salvage and preservation in print of early documents," but also the collection of eyewitness reports, of anecdotes, and of allegedly verbatim accounts of speeches

---

[1] All references to *Richard III* are to the New Folger Shakespeare edition of the play, ed. Barbara A. Mowat and Paul Werstine (New York: Washington Square Press, 1996).

and the like.[2] The compilers of the *Chronicles* would even on occasion publish two incompatible eyewitness accounts of the same event, without privileging one in relation to the other and without trying to construct a single truth about the event through comparison of the accounts.

Rather different protocols are now in place for the representation of history in the editing of *Richard III* and other early modern history plays, many of whose editors appear to be influenced by G. Thomas Tanselle's 1979 essay entitled "External Fact as an Editorial Problem."[3] Adopting a structuralist position, Tanselle sought to establish conventions that editors of any texts whatsoever might employ. Unlike the compilers of Holinshed's *Chronicles*, he presented textual multiplicity as an opportunity for editorial intervention:

> References to external fact raise textual questions because they call attention to a second "text" (the historical fact) with which the text under consideration can be compared. ... The presence in a text of quotations, paraphrases, or references to historical fact undoubtedly raises some perplexing editorial questions; but it also provides editors with a splendid opportunity of demonstrating what critical editing at its most effective can accomplish. (46–47)

As in all his writing, Tanselle advocated editorial establishment of "the text intended by the author at a particular time." Editing, in Tanselle's construction of it, thus becomes a logocentric project if there ever was one; nonetheless, Tanselle's arguments deserve respect for their subtlety, judgment, and sophistication. Discussing references to historical fact, he proceeded advisedly, asking editors first "to consider whether a correction can realistically be undertaken. ... [I]f the erroneous information has been referred to repeatedly or made the basis of further comment, there is no way to make the correction, short of more extensive rewriting and alteration than a scholarly editor can contemplate" (45). What's more, Tanselle did not license editors to make substitutions just because they are possible. He continued:

> But in the case of errors that can feasibly be corrected, the editor must take up the second, and more difficult, kind of consideration, to determine whether or not they *ought* to be corrected. It is here that the editor's critical assessment of all relevant factors is crucial—an assessment of the nature of the sentence and passage where the error occurs, the observed habits of the author, the conventions of the time.

---

[2] (Chicago: Univ. of Chicago Press, 1994), 37, 32–55.
[3] *Studies in Bibliography* 32 (1979): 1–47.

... In a critical edition the treatment of factual errors can be no mechanical matter, covered by a blanket rule. (46, 3)

Poststructuralism has problematized Tanselle's arguments in several related ways. As I have already suggested in citing the protocols employed in Holinshed's *Chronicles*, the citation of detextualized "historical facts" abstracted from documents, anecdotes, etc., is anachronistic for editors of early modern texts. As Bill Ingram has reminded us: "the very etymology of 'fact' should teach us that it is a construct, not a given or *datum*";[4] as constructions, "facts" have been produced under specific historical conditions. In light of Ingram's observation, Tanselle's approach seems curiously ahistorical: he appears to be discussing the whole of editorial practice, but almost all his examples are derived from recent editions of nineteenth-century texts, and he never discusses the treatment of "external fact" across the history of editing. It has a history, as Margreta de Grazia has demonstrated in her work on the late eighteenth-century Shakespeare editor Edmond Malone, whom she credits with developing the practice of regulating and correcting one document—in this case, Shakespeare's plays and poems—with reference to other documents, often, for the history plays, the *Chronicles* of Holinshed and Hall, to which, as Patterson has shown, Malone's very practice was alien. De Grazia's identification of this practice as a production of Malone's own historical context is a bit of an oversimplification—but it may not be much of one because, although there is some evidence of Malone's practice in earlier eighteenth-century Shakespeare editing, Malone pursued the correction of historical fact in Shakespeare with a rigor that exceeds that of any of his predecessors.[5] In this regard Malone continues to be influential upon today's editors in their search for opportunities to bring plays in line with accounts from chronicles.

There have long been attempts to interpret some variants between early printed texts of Shakespeare's plays as evidence that Shakespeare and his contemporaries themselves were interested in making playtexts conform to chronicles. A prominent and, in editions, persistent example comes from *Richard III*. The Folio version once uses three of the names of what for us is a single historical figure as if the three names referred to three different people named Lord Rivers, Lord Woodeville, and Lord Scales:

> First Madam, I intreate true peace of you,
> Which I will purchase with my dutious seruice.

---

[4] *The Business of Playing: The Beginnings of the Adult Professional Theater in Elizabethan London* (Ithaca and London: Cornell Univ. Press, 1992), 19.

[5] *Shakespeare Verbatim* (Oxford: Clarendon Press, 1991), esp. 126–131.

> Of you my Noble Cosin Buckingham,
> If euer any grudge were lodg'd betweene vs.
> Of you and you, Lord *Riuers* and of *Dorset*,
> That all without desert haue frown'd on me:
> Of you Lord *Wooduill*, and Lord *Scales* of you,
> Dukes, Earles, Lords, Gentlemen, indeed of all.
>   (sig. r3v; TLN 1187–1194; 2.1.64–71)[6]

The Quarto version makes no mention of either Lord Woodeville or Lord Scales, since it does not print the Folio line in which these names appear:

> First Madam I intreate true peace of you,
> Which I will purchase with my dutious seruice.
> Of you my noble Coosen Buckingham,
> If euer any grudge were logde betweene vs.
> Of you Lo: Riuers, and Lord Gray of you,
> That all without desert haue frownd on me.
> Dukes, Earles, Lords, gentlemen, indeed of all.
>   (sig. D4–4v)

Even though the Quarto also does not print hundreds of other Folio lines whose absence from the Quarto has never been rationally accounted for, nevertheless a number of scholars and editors have explicitly argued that in this instance some agent excised this single line referring to Woodeville and Scales in the interests of historical accuracy.[7] It may be noted how close this imaginary agent is to the modern scholarly editor in rather unobtrusively nipping out this single line without engaging in any of the substantial rewriting and alteration that is forbidden the contemporary editor by Tanselle. If this imaginary agent were interested in what we have come to regard as historical fact, it is surprising that he would leave so much historical error in the Quarto for later editors to disclose and sometimes also correct. For example, this agent allowed into the Quarto repeated indeterminacy about just how many brothers Queen Elizabeth had—a question intimately related to the Rivers-

---

[6] *The Norton Facsimile: The First Folio of Shakespeare,* 2nd ed. Prepared by Charlton Hinman, with a new introduction by Peter W. M. Blayney (New York: Norton, 1996).

[7] Kristian Smidt, *Iniurious Impostors and* Richard III (New York: Humanities Press, 1964), 98–99; Smidt, *Memorial Transmission and Quarto Copy in* Richard III (New York: Humanities Press, 1970), 42, 44; Anthony Hammond, ed. *King Richard III*, The Arden Shakespeare (London: Methuen, 1981), 17–18; Stanley Wells, Gary Taylor, et al., *William Shakespeare: A Textual Companion* (Oxford: Clarendon Press, 1988), 228–229.

Woodeville–Scales variant just discussed. Sometimes the Quarto gives Elizabeth "brothers"; sometimes it gives Elizabeth only a single "brother." (The Folio, on the other hand, is both consistent and, from our viewpoint, historically accurate in always giving Elizabeth "brothers."[8])

There are so many other examples in *Richard III* of what we would call "historical error" that I have space to mention only those in the first act—all are found in both Quarto and Folio, which, as is usually the case with different early printed versions of the same play, are hardly distinct texts. In both texts, Queen Margaret appears in England after her exile to France, an error that aroused Malone's impatience: "After the battle of Tewksbury, in May, 1471, she was confined in the Tower, where she continued a prisoner till 1475, when she was ransomed ... and removed to France, where she died in 1482. The present scene [that is, 1.3, where Margaret is first onstage] is in 1477–1478. So her introduction in the present scene is a mere poetical fiction" (19: 43). Malone also called attention to the discrepancy between the *Chronicles* and the half-dozen lines in 1.4 in which Clarence protests that he was denied due process before being sentenced to death, lines that could easily have been cut from the Quarto by an agent interested in historical accuracy, but which are nevertheless in the Quarto. According to Malone, "Shakespeare has followed the current tale of his own time, in supposing that Clarence was imprisoned by Edward, and put to death by order of his brother Richard, without trial or condemnation. But the truth is, that he was tried and found guilty by his Peers, and a bill of attainder was afterwards passed against him" (19: 63). As Theobald was first to point out in 1733, the Folio and Quarto texts of *Richard III* are also both in error in calling Lord Stanley the Earl of Derby because he was not "created Earl of Derby until the accession of Henry the Seventh," the event with which the play ends (quoted in Malone 19: 35). Thus Theobald's edition and many following it change Derby to Stanley in stage directions, speech prefixes and dialogue, an easy change metrically, but not one made by the historically minded Quarto agent of modern editorial narrative. Quarto and Folio *Richard III* also share the misrepresentation of Anne as Prince Edward's widow even though, according to so-called historical fact, the two were only betrothed when Edward was killed (Hammond, 35n). Tanselle quite properly counselled editors to have regard to "the observed habits of the author" in assessing whether corrections ought to be made. It is

---

[8] Compare TLN 502, 533, 1465 (not in the Quarto), 2863, 2916, and 3170 (i.e., 1.3.38, 69, 2.3.30, 4.4.94, 147, 400), where the Folio invariably prints "brothers," to the Quarto's sigs. B4, I4, and I4v, where it too has "brothers," and to sigs. B4v and K3, where it inexplicably has "brother."

hard to observe a habit of historical accuracy in the author or in any other agent involved in the publication of *Richard III* in either of its versions.

Tanselle also asked editors to be aware of "the conventions of the time." In assessing these conventions we might look at Massinger's strikingly problematic approach to what we now call historical fact in his 1631 play *Believe as You List*. When he first wrote the play, it was an account of one of the pretenders to the Portuguese throne who had turned up in Italy more than thirty years before near the end of the sixteenth century, claiming to be the lost King Sebastian of Portugal; this pretender had been persecuted and eventually executed by the Spanish. His unfortunate story had been detailed in three pamphlets originally published in English translation at the beginning of the century and never reprinted. Massinger based his play very closely on the pamphlets and on a French source first published in 1605.[9] Massinger included in his play not only the alleged King Sebastian's itinerary in Italy but exact details of his complexion and physical deformities. The censor Henry Herbert forbade production of the play, writing in his office book: "This day being the II of Janu. 1630, I did refuse to allow of a play of Messinger's because itt did contain dangerous matter, as the deposing of Sebastian king of Portugal, by Philip the [Second,] and ther being a peace sworen twixte the kings of England and Spayne."[10] Massinger then rewrote the play—that is, literally reinscribed it; his rewriting is now the only extant version. With help from Edward Knight, book-keeper of the King's Men, Massinger expunged all reference to Portuguese-Spanish affairs, all reference to early modern Europe at all, changed the setting to Asia Minor around 200 BC, made his hero Antiochus the Great, whose name is metrically equivalent to "Sebastian," and left in both the shape and details of the alleged King Sebastian's career.[11] There is then virtually no relation between classical accounts of Antiochus'

---

[9] The identity of Massinger's sources has been known for a long time: see Charles J. Sisson, *Believe as You List by Philip Massinger*, Malone Society Reprints (London: Malone Society, 1927), xvii–xviii; and Philip Edwards and Colin Gibson, eds. *The Plays and Poems of Philip Massinger*, 5 vols. (Oxford: Clarendon Press, 1976), 3: 294–296. Susan MacDonald of the University of Western Ontario has forthcoming an article offering, as one part of its argument, a detailed comparison of the play and its sources.

[10] Joseph Quincy Adams, ed. *The Dramatic Records of Henry Herbert, Master of the Revels, 1623–1673* (Rpt. New York: Blom, [1964]), 19.

[11] For the identification of Knight's hand in the manuscript, see J. Gerritsen, ed. *The Honest Mans Fortune* (Groningen, Djakarta: Wolters, 1952), xxiv.

career and Massinger's play.[12] As Sisson put it in his Malone Society edition
of *Believe as You List*, "Massinger ... apparently endeavoured to save himself
trouble as much as possible" (xix). And so Massinger at first writes a play
about a claimant to the Portuguese throne that is marked by what would be
for us today a high standard of historical accuracy simply because it is based so
closely upon contemporary accounts of this claimant, and then he makes the
play about Antiochus. In changing the names of his setting and his characters,
he produces a text that is utterly unrelated to what we call historical fact.
From this example, it is hard to see how our notion of "historical fact" necessarily has any bite on most editors of early modern English drama.[13]

Massinger and Knight's practice may throw a shadow of doubt over any
editorial presumption that playwrights and acting companies of the early
modern period would seek historical accuracy. Nonetheless, two recent editors of *Henry V* rely to a considerable extent on just such a presumption when
they rename the Dauphin in the play's Agincourt scenes on grounds that history records no Dauphin at the battle.[14] Both these editions are based almost
entirely on the Folio text of the play, the much fuller version in which the
Dauphin is represented at Agincourt; both editors do rely, however, on the
Quarto text for its substitution of the name Bourbon for that of the Dauphin
in the Agincourt scenes. The Quarto's naming is to be preferred, in the view
of these editors, because some agent in the creation of the Quarto was, like
these modern editors, sufficiently attentive to history as to remove the
Dauphin from Agincourt for the reason that there is no chronicle record of
his presence there. For the existence of this kind of agent in the textual
history of *Henry V* there is no more corroborating evidence than there was in

---

[12] For this conclusion I am in part indebted to a paper by Lorin Schwarz presented in my graduate seminar in 1994.

[13] There are notable exceptions, of course, as, for example, in some of Ben
Jonson's work, for which he himself supplied historical documentation.

[14] See Gary Taylor, ed. *Henry V*, The Oxford Shakespeare (Oxford: Clarendon
Press, 1982), esp. 24–26, and Andrew Gurr, ed. *King Henry V*, The New Cambridge
Shakespeare (Cambridge: Cambridge Univ. Press, 1992), esp. 223–225. Editorial sub-
stitution of Bourbon for the Dauphin was initially grounded on analysis of the possible
doubling patterns for staging the Quarto (Stanley Wells and Gary Taylor, *Modernizing
Shakespeare's Spelling* [*With Three Studies in the Text of Henry V*] [Oxford: Clarendon
Press, 1979]) that was seriously called into question by reviewers (See *Shakespeare
Studies* 16 [1983]: 382–391). These editors' massive intervention in the Folio text
seems to me far to exceed anything Tanselle envisioned in his essay. The most recent
editor of *Henry V*, T. W. Craik in the Third Arden series (London: Routledge, 1995),
does not follow Taylor and Gurr, thereby repudiating their assumption that history
plays need to meet standards of historical accuracy.

the case of *Richard III*. Indeed, from the modern point of view of historical accuracy, a persistent failing of Shakespeare's *Henry V*, in both Folio and Quarto, lies in its misnaming of its characters. Both Folio and Quarto misname the Archbishop (of Canterbury) as a bishop. Throughout the play, both use the name Exeter for a character who, in history, did not become Duke of Exeter until after the Battle of Agincourt, which does not take place until the play's fourth act; in history then, there was no Exeter at Agincourt. Both Folio and Quarto give the French herald the name Mountjoy as a proper name when, in "fact," it is not a proper name, but the name of his office. And finally, again throughout the play, both texts employ the name Warwick for a character who, in history, became the Earl of Warwick two years after the Battle of Agincourt—there was no Warwick either at Agincourt. The Quarto compounds this particular historical slip when it expands Warwick's role (Malone 17: 264–265, 370, 440). If there had been some agent involved in the preparation of the *Henry V* Quarto who shared with some of the play's editors an interest in historical accuracy, this agent missed most of his opportunities to act.

For editors who attempt to abstract historical facts from their discursive contexts and then use them to regulate early modern playtexts, perils can sometimes arise because, as Homi Bhabha has observed, history can always only be half made because it is always being made.[15] The ongoing construction, destruction, and reconstruction of history can be observed in the editorial handling of a particular crux in *Henry V*, my last example. As Henry exchanges greetings with the play's French King and Queen in the play's last scene, the French King greets him in the First Folio text of 1623 as "Most worthy brother England," but two lines later the French Queen addresses him as "Brother Ireland" (sig. I6v; TLN 2997, 2999; 5.2.10, 12). The Second Folio of 1632 changes the French Queen's greeting to "Brother England," and it is the Second Folio that has been followed in all subsequent editions of the play until 1995.[16] Editorial allegiance to the Second Folio may seem quite inexplicable since exhaustive study of this Folio earlier this century has revealed that its text has no claim to any authority beyond that of the printing house.[17] Yet this editorial allegiance can be explained with reference to an editorial history that has been made up, albeit rather passively, by the long sequence of Shakespeare editors. First, since the Third Folio is a reprint of the

---

[15] *Nation and Narration* (London: Routledge, 1990), 3.

[16] See *Henry V*, ed. Barbara A. Mowat and Paul Werstine (New York: Washington Square Press, 1995). All references to the play are to this edition.

[17] Matthew W. Black and Matthias A. Shaaber, *Shakespeare's Seventeenth-Century Editors 1632–1685* (New York: MLA and London: Oxford Univ. Press, 1937).

Second, and the Fourth a reprint of the Third, and, further, since Rowe's edition of 1709 is based largely on the Fourth Folio, changes made in the Second Folio had an unimpeded path into the eighteenth century. Then as these readings continued to get reprinted in the next three centuries, repeatedly being put "upon record," they acquired the authority of a cumulative editorial tradition. Now, when there arise editors who represent themselves as editing Shakespeare only to disrupt tradition and thereby somehow make the world a better place, even these self-advertised transgressive editors remain in subjection to and complicit in the making up of tradition.[18]

What distinguishes some contemporary editors from their predecessors are the justifications that they offer for continuing to print traditional but unauthoritative readings. One recent editor takes for granted that in the French Queen's greeting of Henry as "Brother Ireland" the word "Ireland" is a mistake for the word "England" and that the Second Folio's "England" restored the reading of the lost manuscript printer's copy for the First Folio. This editor thus creates a micro-history that will explain how this putative "error" could have arisen. He writes that in the Hand D portion of the play manuscript *The Booke of Sir Thomas More*, which, some scholars have argued, is in Shakespeare's handwriting, the word "England" is spelled with an initial "I." "A similar manuscript spelling," he suggests, "might have misled [the First Folio's] Compositor A into reading it as 'Ireland'" (Gurr, 196).[19] A second recent editor presents another explanation. According to him, "the substitution of 'Ireland' for the clearly required 'England' in '...brother Ireland' seems almost certain to be Shakespeare's own 'Freudian slip'—a slip natural enough in 1599" (Taylor, 18), but a slip that he thinks needs editorial correction—a view mandated by Tanselle, who requires editors to distinguish between authors' unconscious slips and conscious intentions, as if it were possible to do so in an early printed text (2, 34).

I'd like to reflect briefly on how these editorial representations of the word "Ireland" as an error for the word "England" reproduce—I am sure unintentionally—one sixteenth-century English imperial discourse about Ireland. On the assumption or with the conviction that an English king, "brother

---

[18] I am not trying to suggest that it is easy to get out from under editorial tradition. No doubt there are ways I too have blindly followed traditions from which in future I will wish I had extricated myself.

[19] Those editors who fashion palaeographical justifications for emending the Folio's "Ireland" to "England" also invoke the appearance of the word "in-land" in the Folio on sig. h2, TLN 289, 1.2.148. They construct this perfectly good word as an error for "England," an error into which the compositor was allegedly drawn by a putative "Ingland" manuscript spelling (Gurr, 214).

England," cannot also at the same time be "brother Ireland," these editors take for granted that the discursive construction of English national identity in opposition to the Irish was already a completed project by the time of Shakespeare's *Henry V*. As analyzed by Nicholas Canny, Michael Neill, Peter Stallybrass, Ann Rosalind Jones, and Willy Maley among others, this project was one in which the English reserved as exclusive to themselves such traits as godliness, order, civility, and decency by presenting the Irish as errant (like the word "Ireland" in *Henry V*), barbaric (in every sense including "linguistically corrupt"), lawless, subhuman, wild, pagan, even cannibalistic.[20] This discourse in turn justified England's barbaric treatment of the Irish, and something of this barbaric treatment, I acknowledge, is to be found elsewhere in the text of *Henry V*, especially in the characterization of Macmorris. This stage Irishman is ridiculed by the dialogue as barely articulate and not quite intelligible. Michael Neill has argued that Macmorris's very name indicates that his lineage is not to be understood as Gaelic Irish; rather he is to be thought of as a degenerate descendant of the medieval Anglo–Norman invaders of Ireland, who were assimilated by the Gaelic Irish: "Captain Macmorris [is] an 'Irishman' whose hybrid surname and savage temper reveal him as an exemplar of that 'bastardlike' degeneracy to which English conquerors were prone [in one imperial discourse] in the 'Land of Ire'" (19). If Macmorris constituted the sole representation of Ireland in the play and if there were only a single discourse of Ireland at the play's time, then it would seem unlikely that Henry could be greeted in the play as "brother Ireland." Editors might in such circumstances have grounds for representing the reading "brother Ireland" as a degeneration of "brother England." Whether the alleged textual degeneration from "England" to "Ireland" took place in the bog of Shakespeare's unconscious or in the slovenliness of the otherwise precise Compositor A, this linguistic degeneration would be analogous to the alleged degeneration of the transplanted English-Irish Macmorris.[21]

---

[20] Canny, "The Theory and Practice of Acculturation: Ireland in a Colonial Context," in *Kingdom and Colony: Ireland in the Atlantic World 1560–1800* (Baltimore: Johns Hopkins Univ. Press, 1988), 31–68; Neill, "Broken English and Broken Irish: Nation, Language, and the Optic Power in Shakespeare's Histories," *Shakespeare Quarterly* 45 (1994), 1–32; Stallybrass and Jones, "Dismantling Irena: The Sexualizing of Ireland in Early Modern England," in *Nationalisms and Sexualities*, ed. Andrew Parker et al. (New York: Routledge, 1992), 157–171; Maley, "Shakespeare, Holinshed, and Ireland: Resources and Con-texts," forthcoming. I am grateful to Dr. Maley for the opportunity to read his essay in manuscript.

[21] For Compositor A's precision, see Alice Walker, "The Folio Text of *1 Henry IV*," *Studies in Bibliography* 6 (1954): 45–59.

But the English othering of Ireland was not yet complete in the sixteenth century; it was, in Homi Bhabha's phrase, only half made up. What's more, the othering of Ireland was not the only English imperial discourse of Ireland at the time of *Henry V* or in *Henry V* itself. Instead, the othering of Ireland was crossed by a contradictory discourse of English desire for the assimilation of Ireland, and for the identification of England with Ireland. Sir John Davies presented this second imperial discourse of Ireland in his *Discoverie of the Trve Cavses why Ireland was neuer entirely Subdued* (1612) as he looked forward to a time in the very near future when English justice will have

> reclaymed the Irish from their wildnesse, caused them to cut off their Glibs and long Haire; to conuert their Mantles into Cloaks; to conform themselues to the maner of *England* in al their behauiour and outward formes. ... as we may conceiue an hope, that the next generation will in tongue & heart, and euery way else, becom *English*, so as there will bee no difference or distinction, but the Irish Sea betwixt us. (sigs. Mm2–2v)

Pride of possession of an Ireland imagined to be assimilated into a growing English empire is also available to be read in *Henry V*. Henry woos Katherine with this offer, "England is thine, Ireland is thine, France is thine" (5.2.248–249), the scheme of asyndeton reducing what have since become independent nations to equal status as possessions of the English crown.[22] In this second discourse, the history in which Ireland will have become the opposite against which England will have defined itself as a nation has not yet been made up—not made up, that is, until editors—mistakenly to my mind—make it up when they change "brother Ireland" to "brother England." In the unemended Folio text there is room for an Irish reader to construct a position from which to read the text as imputing value to Ireland—even if only as an English possession; from the Second Folio and all subsequent editions, the Irish reader is arbitrarily excluded, just as she has been excluded from so much of the history of Ireland subsequently made up in English discourse.

Tanselle's call to editors to have regard for external fact may raise some intractable problems for editors of early modern playtexts, who may have difficulty reducing these texts to the singularity of "historical fact," when the texts belong to an age in which history was compiled with regard to the plurality of sources and voices through which it was preserved. So it may be

---

[22] Compare *The True Tragedie of Richard the third* (London, 1594): "Henry the seuenth, by the grace of God, King of England, *France*, and Lord of *Ireland*" (sig. H4v).

necessary for editors of these playtexts to conceive of *history* as *histories* in the manner of the new historicism that has followed in the wake of post-structuralism. The validity of this advisory is independent of the validity of my example from *Henry V*. What I am suggesting is revising editorial protocols, not discarding them. Since Shakespeareans continue to use modern editions even after poststructuralist critiques of them, it would seem to the point to modify and improve the protocols of editing in the light of ongoing historicist scholarship.

Preposterous Poststructuralism:
Editorial Morality and the
Ethics of Evidence

STEVEN URKOWITZ

S EVERAL MAJOR OPPORTUNITIES FOR EDITING AFTER POSTSTRUC-
turalism, I believe, arise from thinking about Shakespearean playscripts
as tentative or ad hoc suggestions for performances, and editing the
multiple-text plays such as *King Lear* or *Romeo and Juliet* may perhaps best be
approached as opportunities for editors to offer alternative suggestions for different performances on different occasions with different actors and audiences.

In his important essay " 'Foul Papers' and 'Bad' Quartos" (*Shakespeare
Quarterly* 41 [1990], 64–86), Paul Werstine suggests that a truly poststructuralist approach to Shakespearean multiple-text plays would be to construct "a
narrative that includes post-structuralist differential readings of multiple text
works." Such a narrative, he suggests, should "keep in play not only multiple
readings and versions but also the multiple and dispersed agencies that could
have produced the variants" (86). In practice, however, constructing narratives
about plays is not necessarily the same as generating editions of plays, or developing scripts to use in productions of plays. Though it might be. Poststructuralist editors of Shakespeare (or indeed editors of any critical persuasion)
now have both thrilling opportunities and awesome responsibilities to invent
ways of celebrating the recognizably dispersed authorities of documentary
evidence, editorial tradition, and contemporary judgment. Creating a singular
"authoritative" text for general readers will all too likely perpetuate misap-
prehensions of all artistic processes and particularly the communal production

of dramatic art within densely figured historical communities such as Shakespeare's.

I would like to explore one very small textual occasion I believe invites imaginative editing of the poststructuralist kind: a single moment in *King Lear*. I've written about it before (*Shakespeare's Revision of King Lear* [1980], 38–40). Like my predecessor in the reformer's trade, Lemuel Gulliver, I had hoped the timely publication of my observations would have brought about some salutary and immediate amendment among the practitioners of editorial arts and crafts. But, as many of my friends had warned, in the past fifteen years my proposed reforms have not yet been much realized in contemporary editions. Unlike Lemuel Gulliver I nevertheless continue to be hopeful. I continue to cajole my editorial colleagues. And also I may yet encourage some editorially smitten, energetic, and otherwise unemployed young scholars. Perhaps one or two young men or women will leap into what I feel should prove an exciting and rewarding task: an expansive and generously poststructural editing of Shakespeare.

As bait I offer an enticing example, taken from the opening scene of the 1608 Quarto and 1623 First Folio texts of *King Lear*. Kent has been banished for his intemperate loyalty; he bids a jaunty farewell to the King and court, and he exits the stage. With no intervening events indicated in either of the scripts, the Earl of Gloucester escorts onstage France and Burgundy, suitors for Cordelia. Here is the Quarto text:

> Thus Kent O Princes, bids you all adew,
> Heele shape his old course in a countrie new.
> *Enter France and Burgundie with Gloster.*
> *Glost.* Heers France and Burgundie my noble Lord.
>
> (Q1 B3–B3v)

The Folio version of the same passage reads:

> Thus Kent, O Princes, bids you all adew,
> Hee'l shape his old course, in a Country new. *Exit.*
> **Flourish.** *Enter Gloster with France, and Burgundy, At-*
> *tendants.*
> *Cor.* Heere's France and Burgundy, my Noble Lord.
>
> (TLN 200–204)

The texts present two dramatically significant differences, both with interesting consequences affecting a stage enactment of the passage should the scripts be used to govern performances. (Here is my local definition for "dramatic significance": a textual variant is dramatically significant if a person who doesn't understand the language nevertheless could observe differences in performances of the alternative versions.) The first significant variant is *"Flourish"* only in the Folio stage direction. The second: the speech-prefix *"Glost."* in the Quarto appears as *"Cor."* in the Folio.

First, a poststructural editor trying to make sense out of the divergent evidence should, I believe, invent a way to signal to readers the possible theatrical effect of the flourish, which does not appear in Q. After the heraldic trumpets announced the entry of King Lear earlier in the scene, the Quarto's *"No flourish"* indicates the sound of one hand clapping, a hugger-mugger omission of celebratory music appropriate to high nobility moving through ceremonially charged space. In our own roles as editors responsible for presenting *King Lear* to readers perhaps unfamiliar with theatrical scripts, we might help such readers imagine or even encourage them to assay in a rehearsal-room or classroom differential enactments of this moment that would propel live actors into the scene with fictional energy and recognizably familiar purpose.

Of course, we can't know why the "Flourish" call does not appear in the Quarto. We cannot tell if "Shakespeare the Bard" added the *Flourish* that shows up in the Folio or chopped it out of whatever manuscript stood behind the Quarto. We can't tell if the Royal Trumpeter who picked up extra money doing gigs at the Globe made the suggestion, or even if, on one exuberant spring day, he ad-libbed the vivid trumpet call and then someone thought to write it into the script that later became the Folio. We don't know if Globe theatre performances of *Lear* always had the trumpet flourish because someone told the trumpeter, once, orally, but forgot to write it into the script until after the Quarto was printed. And we don't know if, perhaps, in the Globe theatre they never had the flourish at all despite the instruction printed in the Folio. Maybe the journeyman compositor in Nathanial Butter's printing house left it out of the Quarto, or maybe the apprentice Folio compositor in Jaggard's shop fifteen years later in a fit of musical expansiveness plunked it in. We don't know.

But thought is free, and a poststructural editor could include on her multimedia CD-ROM a few all-purpose trumpet calls. Imagine an icon to click that would promptly supply the reader of the CD-ROM with, say, Wynton Marsalis playing a Renaissance flourish on a Renaissance instrument. Or even in a low-budget, simple ink-and-paper edition, a poststructural editor could coach her readers about possible actions that would realize the variant performative potentialities of this textual variant.

Imagine that an editor suggests to her readers that, in the fiction of the play, the characters onstage quickly comprehend the dismal prospects of the forthcoming nuptial conversations. Any character with such knowledge could signal the trumpeter to hold off a conventional celebratory fanfare. Imagine if

Goneril were to make such a move. Or if King Lear imperiously warns off
the trumpets. Or if Cordelia gestures for silence. Actors love to perform such
actions onstage; Shakespeare's scripts are so beloved by actors in no small
degree because they encourage such imaginable and playful doings. They
would be fun to try out, adopt, or discard, and a poststructural edition of the
play well might encourage such trials in an effort to underscore the tentative
and experimental parameters of theatrical scripts in their most practical and
professional uses. Such play of possibilities may or may not alter the "meaning" of *King Lear* on an abstract scale, but the trumpet or its absence can
intensely affect an actor's and audience's experience of the moment.

To pre- and postmodern editors, a more problematic textual variant arises
where the speech prefix reading "*Glost.*" in the Quarto appears as "*Cor.*" in
the Folio. The alternative scripts give interesting possibilities to consider and
to play with.

Who will speak the line that will move the action forward? Gloucester?
"Cor." for Cornwall? Or maybe even "Cor." for Cordelia? Suppose that the
words are said by the character indicated in the Quarto text, the salacious Earl
of Gloucester, he of the foul mouth and slippery codpiece? Suppose as one
possibility Gloucester enters as the happy usher of the two noble suitors.
Leading this short parade of dignitaries, Gloucester may not have heard about
Cordelia's disgrace. Considering momentarily a jaunty Gloucester as master of
ceremonies, we may recall a parallel theatrical moment in *Troilus and Cressida*
when lecherous Pandarus oversees the first interview between that pair of
potential bedfellows. Here the actor playing jolly old Gloucester—soon to be
called "blind Cupid"—may well be thinking about these lucky nobles at
"good sport" with Cordelia. "Here's France and Burgundy, my noble Lord."
Or suppose that Gloucester has been warned by a servant or a courtier who
may have been sent out earlier by Lear: "Call France. Who stirs? Call Burgundy." Gloucester may in that case speak his line as a helpless ameliorator, as
we see him later saying to Lear, "I would have all well betwixt you" (TLN
1396). "Here's France and Burgundy, my noble Lord."

And we have an alternative textual possibility: this same action is introduced into Lear's consciousness not by Gloucester, as is directed by the
Quarto speech prefix, but instead by Cordelia or by the Duke of Cornwall.
One of the possible speakers suggested by the Folio text, Cornwall was just
enfranchised with half the rich dowry earlier planned for Cordelia and one of
these suitors. Following the Folio as a script to govern and to suggest stage
action, we may imagine for a moment that King Lear has turned himself away
from the upstage doors on the Globe platform. Perhaps he is looking away to
avoid crossing glances with departing Kent. The trumpet flourishes, the suitors
enter, led by or followed by Gloucester either forewarned or just now

noticing that the expected ardor for greeting the suitors has cooled terribly.

We may imagine that Cornwall at this moment enjoys the potential discomfiture of France and Burgundy, since he already has so benefited from their loss. He's that kind of guy. And we may well imagine that he takes pleasure in calling the King's attention to the "unfinished business" of Cordelia's marriage now so ineluctably at hand. The actor playing Cornwall knows how he will soon become the eye-popping Cornwall, the sadistic mutilator of old men, the Cornwall who embraces Bastard Edmund as a true father. The players onstage, including Cornwall, can load their apprehension of the moment with their particular reactions to this noble vexillator who presses France and Burgundy into Lear's consciousness. "Here's France and Burgundy, my noble Lord."

And finally we may consider a reading of the Folio text where Cordelia announces the arrival of the men come to take her away from her kind nursery. Again, we must imagine the moment. Kent departs, the suitors and Gloster arrive, and, further, we may imagine that all other figures on the stage say nothing even after the indicated heraldic trumpet-call fades into echo. And we may imagine further that Lear—unlike his peremptory command when he first enters the audience's view: "Attend the lords of France and Burgundy, Gloucester"—silently chooses *not* to attend the lords of France and Burgundy. Following the authority of the Folio version of the script, COR[delia] well may speak these words. Everything we know (or more to the point, everything an actor playing the role of Cordelia knows) about Cordelia makes her also a plausible speaker here. Earlier she stood up to her father in the face of his wrath. The actor playing the role knows that in a few hours on the same stage, in order to restore her father to his proper status, she will lead an army in his defense, not a task for a limp, frail vessel without daring or initiative. And at this moment, an actor playing Cordelia within the fictional circumstances of the play may consider how delay in greeting the suitors would negatively affect the King's dignity among the nations as well as her own marriage prospects. A poststructural edition of the play should include among the alternative possibilities offered by its underlying documents a prompt for the actor to take charge of a stalled action. "Here's France and Burgundy, my noble Lord."

Actors and directors of necessity think about stage action in these ways: entrances and exits and the imaginative and narrative possibilities they can be woven into. Our students and our colleagues should be encouraged to think in these ways also. These three alternative speakers highlight an indeterminate, unfixed quality in the scripts.

According to different narratives I've read over the years, textual scholars have argued that actors may have made these changes, or playhouse scribes, or illicit transcribers, printing-house compositors, playhouse officials, or later revising playwrights not associated with whoever may have done any earlier work on the play. The theater historian Gerald Eades Bentley proposes that the playhouse author of the King's Men acting company may have been ideally situated and even contractually obligated to make such changes as well. Any or all these agents may have contributed to the underlying documents finally gone to press in Okes's and Jaggard's printing houses.

Despite claims to the contrary, I believe that the indicated fluidities and instabilities of extant texts revealed by examination of the evidentiary documents ought not lead to any abdication of professional imagination on the part of contemporary textual editors. Given the multiple possibilities of the stage direction and speech prefix we have been examining, informed editors should, I believe, somehow find ways to inform their readers as well that multiple narratives exist both for explaining the history of the documents and for explaining the actions encoded in those documents. But this has not been easy to accomplish in the past; it is not a simple task even granting the insights about authorship offered by poststructuralism; and it will not be easy in any future editorial enterprise—however well supported by print or multimedia technologies.

Old habits die hard, and traditional editorial authority seems to encourage unwarranted textual massage even in projects meant to respond directly to poststructuralist challenges. René Weis, *King Lear: A Parallel Text Edition* (1992) gives readers a "corrected" version of the Quarto and a parallel text of the Folio. The speech prefix "Cor." is one of the variants he "corrects" in his version of the Folio. He explains: "I have changed F's *Cor.* to Q's *Gloucester*, who was sent to attend France and Burgundy and now introduces them." But no dramaturgical necessity or principle *requires* that a character sent on an errand must accomplish every or even any aspect of the task before returning to the stage. Rules of dramatic narration need not follow syllogistic determinism. Weis claims that with his edition a reader can "engage directly with the problems raised by the two texts of *King Lear* and consider current thinking about the play" (back cover copy), but his editorial intervention seriously prejudices precisely the kinds of inquiry he would invite.

In what initially seems a more postmodern effort, the editors of the New Folger Library *King Lear*, Barbara Mowat and Paul Werstine, repeatedly challenge the possibility of knowing the relationship of the evidentiary documents to "the historical figure" of Shakespeare. As their copy text, the New Folger editors explain that they "choose F not because we believe that it stands in closer relation to Shakespeare than Q1 (we do not think it possible to establish which of Q1 or F is closer to the historical figure Shakespeare)." Despite such poststructural skepticism in the face of what they consider to be indeterminate evidence, the New Folger editors slide—perhaps inadvertently in a moment of pre-modern nostalgia for the lost golden age—back into basing some of their choices upon a hypothetically determinable idealized text. They choose as the speech prefix for their edition the word "*Gloucester*" rather than the abbreviation "*Cor.*" because here and in two other places "Q1 supplies a word that coheres with the story." They continue: "We print a word from Q1 rather than from F when a word from F seems at odds with *the story* that *the play* tells and Q1 supplies a word that coheres with *the story*" (lxiii; emphasis supplied).

This momentary eruption of both a singularly Platonic "play" and an equally singular Platonic abstraction at a further remove called "the story that the play tells" vaults us back to the old pre-poststructuralist worlds of Authorial Intentions and Lost Idealized Forms. The documentary evidence appropriately celebrated as the source for the New Folger edition thereby languishes. These editors replace the authority of the de-centered author not with the authority of evidence but rather with the authority of "*the* story that *the* play tells" as it is defined by the editors. And far more than in most other plays that exist only in single authoritative texts, the multiple versions of *King Lear* starkly demonstrate that each individual script is not "*the* story." Each individual reading will generate its own "story" as the variant words suggest actions and personal references to actors and audiences. Old-style authoritarian editing easily co-opts the liberatory potentialities of poststructuralism.

Nevertheless, elsewhere in their edition of *King Lear*, Werstine and Mowat gracefully lay out what may be considered ideal goals of studying (and editing) Shakespearean texts, an editorial morality worthy of their high enterprise:

> It is immensely rewarding to work carefully with Shakespeare's language so that the words, the sentences, the wordplay, and the implied stage action all become clear—as readers for the past four centuries have discovered. ... [T]he joy of being able to stage one of Shakespeare's plays in one's imagination, to return to passages that continue to yield further meanings (or further questions) the more one reads them—these are pleasures that, for many, rival (or at least augment) those of the performed text, and certainly make it worth the considerable effort to "break the code" of Elizabethan poetic drama and let free the remarkable language that makes up a Shakespeare text. (xxx)

To encourage such accomplishment, however, postmodern editing ought to take the now theoretically justifiable path of inventing ways to encourage visualization of multiple textual possibilities. I've argued elsewhere that the major benefit of studying the variant texts of multiple-text plays is that juxtaposed staging schemes such as the entrance of the suitors in *King Lear* 1.1 lead students to see and to think about words and bodies in action. Postmodern editors trying to help students visualize that action might consider adapting page layouts more appropriate to the contending authoritative documents that make up what we call *King Lear*. But the point of any contrastive exercise shouldn't be to replace the older moralistic rigidities of a single "good" text with newer but equally rigid claims for "two good texts" or even three or nineteen.

We need looser formats, with larger pages, perhaps something with magazine-style sidebars that would allow an editor to spin out a discussion of a twenty-line textual variant or a particularly apposite antecedent source text. Editions could benefit from a bounty of imaginative treats for readers stashed in page margins: alternative stage and costume designs, or even thumbnail sketches indicating possible blocking or massing of players on a stage.

Provided with portfolios of such images generously supplied from a variety of sources and readily referenced within a reading text, readers of a poststructuralist edition might better learn how to visualize creatively the multidimensional stage experiences that stage scripts regulate. Then we all could be surprised and delighted to see on stage and in our minds' recreations a rich variety of images accompanying and framing these words—"Here's France and Burgundy, my noble Lord."—as well as the thousands of other words and actions in Shakespearean scripts.

Judgment

GARY TAYLOR

W E DON'T HAVE MUCH TIME. BUT YOU DECIDED TO SPEND some of the little time you have left listening to me, and I decided to spend rather more of the little time I have left thinking about what I might have to tell you which would be worth this portion of our lives. I could find only ten things to say. First:

We have to choose. You had to choose whether to come to this convention; having come, you had to choose which session, if any, to attend. All around us, people are choosing whom to hire, and which books to buy. You cannot hire them all or buy them all or hear them all.

You also cannot edit everything. Even I cannot edit everything. So you must choose what to edit. If you choose to edit the Collected Works of Thomas Middleton, then you have to choose whether to include *The Revenger's Tragedy*, whether to exclude *The Family of Love*. If you are the general editor, you have to make hundreds of choices: about editorial procedures, about contributors, about texts, about persons. If you are editing a single text, you must make choices about every word, every punctuation mark, in that text. When you encounter, in *The Widow*, the phrase "to court me bodly," you have to decide whether to leave this piece of apparent nonsense, or to emend it, as everyone has done since the middle of the eighteenth century, to "boldly," assuming that the compositor omitted an "l"; or whether to emend it to something else, for instance, "bodily," assuming that the compositor omitted an "i."

In *The Merchant of Venice*, there are three caskets; Portia's suitors have to choose one. Valeria, the title character in *The Widow*, has three suitors; she can marry only one. Editors, critics, theorists, suitors, those to whom they sue, we are all, as Middleton says, "bound to make choice," forced to be free. But—and this is my second observation—

Our choices are limited. Sometimes we face only what is described, in *A Trick to Catch the Old One*, as "a choice of stinks." Valeria gets the man that she wants, but he is a spendthrift who has, by his own account, lusted after a thousand women. Such a man is inconceivable as the hero of a Shakespearean comedy. We can imagine a world in which Valeria gets a better husband. Or we can imagine a world in which Valeria, rather than having to choose just one suitor, could have all three (say, one for money, one for friendship, one for sex): there are, after all, polyandrous human societies. We can all posit protocols and boundaries more desirable than those that prevail in our own time and place—that is what the utopian fictions of Thomas More, Francis Bacon, and Margaret Cavendish do, imagine new and better rules. But any protocols or boundaries which we can imagine will inevitably limit choice. Furthermore, even within the geometrically circumscribed realm of choice defined by those rules, choices will be further limited by unplanned concatenations of events. Elizabeth Cary wrote at least two plays, but we can teach only one of them, because only one of them has survived.

What is true of ourselves, as teachers and readers, is also true of Renaissance women. Their choices were limited by boundaries, protocols, arbitrary concatenations of events—birth, class, geography, education, nationality, race. They were also, of course, limited by the protocols of gender. Women were not admitted to universities in early modern England; women were not allowed to perform in public theaters; women could not become apprentices in the printing business, and could not own or run a printing press unless they inherited it from a deceased husband.

The choices of early modern women were limited by, among other things, the fact that they were women. But although early modern English women had fewer choices than men, they still did have choices, there were options available to them, and if they came from certain families they had quite a few options. They could choose, just as we can choose. But—and this is my third observation—

We do not want to choose. We may not like any of the options available to us. Even if we like the options, to choose one option is to forego all others, and there is always something to be said for the options we forego. We cannot be sure which is the right alternative; if we were sure, there would be no problem of choice. And the consequences of misjudgment can be disastrous. If Portia's suitors choose the wrong casket, they must leave immediately and remain permanently celibate. If Valeria chooses the wrong suitor, she may be miserable for the rest of her life. If, as an editor, you publish a poem attributed to Shakespeare in a seventeenth-century manuscript, you may, for the rest of your life, be accused of a complete lack of literary judgment. Choice is both appealing and frightening: "it doth require," as the White Queen's Pawn realizes in *A Game at Chess*, "it doth require a meeting 'twixt my fear and my desire." To choose is to commit ourselves, and thereby to expose ourselves, and therefore—

We do not want to choose. That is one reason most people prefer Shakespeare to Middleton. We are particularly attracted to fictions in which we do not have to choose, in which we can have our cake and eat it too. Shakespeare is exceptionally adept at giving us goodnesses that are, outside the theater, sadly incompatible. Bassanio chooses the leaden casket; unlike the other suitors, he is not swayed by "outward shows," the external lures of gold or silver, beauty or wealth. But of course Portia *is* beautiful and *is* rich. Bassanio recognizes that "The world is still deceived with ornament," and for his moral rectitude he is rewarded with—an ornamental woman, whose inward worth just happens to be reflected in her body and her bank account. The moral principle articulated by the scene is incompatible with the narrative logic of the scene, but our experience of the scene tells us that we can have morality *and* money, a deep spiritual love contemptuous of the mere physical world *and* a great body to fuck. We don't have to choose.

Again and again, Shakespeare tells us stories in which we do not have to choose. Petruccio manages to be both feared and loved—a combination which, as Machiavelli well knew, cannot be sustained, in even the most politic reign. Hamlet is a multiple murderer, but he apologizes to Laertes, explaining that it was not Hamlet but "his madness" that was responsible for all the havoc; flights of angels sing the killer to his rest, and he is borne nobly and ceremoniously from the stage, while centuries of spectators weep, and pride themselves on their little resemblances to that "sweet prince." Othello murders his wife, but the blame for that is shifted to the seemingly omnipotently evil Iago, just as the blame for Hamlet's carnage is shifted to his madness; so at the end Othello can epitomize a man who "loved . . . too well," and die kissing, with our tearful approbation, the woman he has just strangled. Henry V is a conqueror of kingdoms and a nice guy, a very charming rapist. Oldcastle—or Falstaff: you have to choose what to call him—Sir John praises sack, and spends most of his free time drinking in a tavern, but he is not an alcoholic. Prospero catalogues the triumphs of his "so potent art," but in the same speech he abjures his "rough magic" and promises to drown his book: we get the tingly pleasures of unrestrainable power, immediately combined with the pleasures of moral restraint. We do not have to choose between exacting obedience and earning love, we do not have to choose between revenge and self-respect, we do not have to choose between killing a woman and loving her, we do not have to choose between conqueror and comforter, we do not have to choose between an alcoholic high and a healthy body, we do not have to choose between our fantasies of omnipotence and our fantasies of righteousness.

But Middleton's characters and Middleton's audiences are not allowed this delicious suspension of the necessity for choice. *The Revenger's Tragedy* answers *Hamlet*, by reminding us of the choice Shakespeare obscures. Vindice gets his revenge, but in order to be able to do that he has to choose to become a revenger, become someone who deserves to be executed, someone virtually indistinguishable from those he condemns. Falstaff drinks, but Dampit in *A Trick to Catch the Old One* is unmistakably an alcoholic, probably the first real alcoholic in English literature, terminally deteriorating from the physical effects of his addiction. Whorehound wants Mrs. Allwit to be unfaithful to her husband, but also wants her to be faithful to Whorehound himself, and so is tormented by jealousy, and eventually abandoned. In *Women Beware Women* Leantio wants a woman so alluring that men want to steal her, a woman moreover who enjoys being wanted, a woman who consequently acquiesces, even collaborates, in being stolen; but these very qualities, which attracted him to Bianca, guarantee that he will not be able to keep Bianca. Leantio wants Bianca, but doesn't want her to *be* Bianca. Isabella wants to hump her uncle, but doesn't want him to *be* her uncle. The Duke wants another man's wife, but doesn't want to *be* an adulterer. All these people want "the fatness of their desires," including their "desires of goodness."

Shakespeare gives us what we impossibly want, and the world loves him for it; Middleton shows us what we impossibly want, and most of us prefer not to see. The art of both playwrights derives much of its power from the fact that human beings do not want to choose.

But in life—that is, outside of the plays of Shakespeare—we do have to choose, even though we don't want to. Consequently—and this is my fourth observation—

We prefer to let someone else choose for us. Portia lets her father's lottery choose a husband for her. Editors rush to adopt, to impose upon themselves, rules formulated by Fredson Bowers or W. W. Greg or G. Thomas Tanselle or Jerome McGann or some other guru, rules that scientifically determine the choice of control-text, the choice of variant, the layout of page and apparatus. Conservatives and self-styled radicals alike accept traditional attributions, make a principle of accepting every choice made, consciously or unconsciously, by an anonymous seventeenth-century compositor or scribe. The new series of

Shakespeare Originals advertises itself as a radically independent alternative, but in fact it blindly accepts the textual choices made by other people as well as the canonical choices made by other people. As editors, we let publishers choose what we will edit, by accepting their commissions to edit popular works—that is, works that have already been edited again and again. As teachers, we let other people's choices about which texts to edit determine which texts we order for our classes. We teach what we were taught, or we teach the courses that have always been taught in this department, or we teach the courses that are fashionable this year or this decade. We teach what others have edited, what others have taught or are teaching. We let tradition choose a canon for us, or we let fashion choose a canon for us.

Why should we do this? Why should we let other people choose for us? Because—and this is my fifth observation—

If someone else chooses for us, we can deny that we have made a choice. If the choice is wrong, it is someone else's fault. As editors and as critics and as teachers, we can attribute our choices to the invisible hand of the market, or the judgment of the ages. By not exercising, we do not expose, our own judgment. In fact, we can righteously condemn anyone who does make such a choice, by calling attention to the arrogance of that person's behavior. It does take a great deal of arrogance to do B, when everyone else is doing A; and arrogance is not a virtue. That is itself one of the choices we sometimes have to make: whether to be admirably modest, and therefore perhaps acquiesce in a mistake other people are also making, or to refuse to acquiesce in what we think is wrong— an independence we can only achieve by being or becoming arrogant about our own powers of judgment. It is, I know, arrogant of me to prefer, as I often do, Middleton to Shakespeare; it is arrogant of me even to treat them as equals, despite the judgment of four hundred years of critics and audiences. Those who accept Shakespeare's canonical status, those who go on endlessly re-editing and re-interpreting him, those who relegate Thomas Middleton or Lucy Hutchins to the sidelines, do not usually believe they are making a choice; they believe that they are accepting a fact, the fact that the world has preferred and still prefers Shakespeare, a fact which only a madman (that is, someone like me) would deny.

But—and this is my sixth observation—

We have to choose whether to accept other people's choices. To acquiesce is to choose. That was, after all, the judgment of Nuremberg. It is also a judgment Middleton often passes on his characters. Bianca in *Women Beware Women* was raped; I don't doubt that; she did not want or choose to be sexually ambushed by the Duke. But, eventually, she acquiesces in her status as his mistress, and then his bride. She becomes guilty, in the end, simply by accepting a choice, a fact, someone else imposed upon her. She chooses not to choose; she lets herself be chosen, just as Portia lets herself be chosen by whoever picks the right casket. Middleton expects us to condemn the woman who surrenders her choice; Shakespeare, by contrast, expects us to applaud the woman who surrenders her choice. In fact, Shakespeare tells us that, by surrendering her choice, Portia gets her choice: her father's mechanism, in which she acquiesces, drives away a whole series of undesirable suitors, rewarding the one suitor she desires. Once again, Shakespeare tells us that we don't have to choose—we can acquiesce in other people's choices, *and* get exactly what we want. But perhaps I should not say "we," because I am male, and Portia is female. Shakespeare tells us, more precisely, that *a woman* can acquiesce in *men's* choices, and thereby get exactly what she wants. Middleton does not gender issues of choice in this way. As he puts it in *The Nice Valour*, "desire is of both genders," and he writes in *More Dissemblers* of "the desire of both sexes." Lady Mary Wroth would have agreed with Middleton. In *Love's Victory*, her female protagonist has her marital fate determined by her dead "father's will," but unlike Shakespeare's Portia, Wroth's Musella does not acquiesce in the arrangement; she chooses instead to commit suicide.

But this difference in the gendering of choice and acquiescence is only a part of the larger relationship between choice and identity—which leads to my seventh observation—

We are what we choose. Portia IS an acquiescent woman. She acquiesces in her father's choice of marriage mechanism; once correctly chosen by Bassanio, she announces her complete submission to his husbandly authority; in Venice, she is the acquiescent voice of the law, speaking not with her own authority but as the mouthpiece of an absent male expert, forcing the Jew to acquiesce, reducing him to a status of abjection below even a woman.

But it is not just Portia who is what she chooses. So are we. So am I. For nineteen years *Henry V* has been one of my favorite plays; watching it again last month I realized with some horror that my fondness for that play, for that story of a cold-blooded self-righteous organizer of havoc who has at the same time "a good heart" and is irresistibly likeable, that my *choice* of that play says something about me; that it is not entirely accidental that people have so often, in describing my career, used military metaphors. What does it say about *me* that the last five minutes of *Hamlet* or of *Othello* have always moved me to tears? More generally, what does our collective canonization of Shakespeare, our choice of or acquiescence in his work, say about *us* as a culture? The culture that has deified Shakespeare is the culture that believes we can cut taxes *and* balance the budget, the culture of beer commercials without alcoholics, the culture of Hollywood, the culture whose most abiding foundational belief is that everyone can have it all.

But of course that is not "us." We look at the traffic jams, the pollution, the overdevelopment, the frantic personal schedules, the poverty, crime, chemical dependence, sexual exploitation, racism, stupidity, irrelevance, and we say "That is not *me*. That is not *us*." And who has taught us to distinguish, so confidently, between our social choices and our real selves? Shakespeare, among others. It is not just Iago who says "I am not what I am." When Hamlet or Othello disclaims responsibility for his crimes, including his crimes against a woman who loves him, he is asserting the foundational goodness of a private motionless self that can be neatly separated from its dubious public choices. When Shakespeare's women dress as men, we are always made aware, beneath the veneer of their male actions, of their underlying substantive femaleness. Indeed, cross-dressing is, for Shakespeare, simply a subset of the larger trope of disguise, which he uses more obsessively than any other dramatist. The social world may be fooled by the actions of Rosalind and Viola, Richard III and Iago, but we are never fooled. Shakespeare persuades us that his characters have—and therefore that we have—an interior true self, insulated from our choices in the social world.

Some of Middleton's characters share that belief. Beatrice-Joanna, in *The Changeling*, is convinced she is a good person, despite having hired a hit-man to dispose of her fiancé. But DeFlores insists, the play insists, that she is "the deed's creature," the product of her choices.

We, in turn, are the canon's creatures. We become the texts we choose to canonize, or the texts in whose canonization we choose to acquiesce. Because—and this is my eighth observation—

In choosing a person, we choose their choices. In her "choice of men," according to Middleton and Dekker's *The Patient Man and the Honest Whore*, a woman is making a "choice of beards, choice of legs, and choice of every, every, every thing." That final *thing* is, of course, partly a genital thing. But the word "thing" tends to reify what is, in fact, an action. Beards can be cut many different ways, legs can be displayed in as many different ways. What attracts us to another person is a set of behaviors: the way they laugh, talk, walk, think, shave, behave. Even physical attraction depends upon response to a set of behaviors: any good actor or actress knows that you can make yourself look beautiful or not, sexy or not, and for women particularly but not exclusively, making yourself as beautiful as possible was, and still is, a personal imperative, a social obligation, aided and abetted by clothes, cosmetics, conduct books. Beauty is always performed; beauty is always a choice; and those performances and choices always operate within the system of conventions, boundaries, and protocols that determines what, in a given time and place, counts as beautiful. Beauty, proverbially, is in the eye—the visual organ, and the ego—of the beholder.

Aesthetic judgment, of course, is, in one way or another, a judgment that something is beautiful, an attraction to the choices made by a performing artist. In deciding that a piece of writing is beautiful, or powerful, or subtle, or whatever words we choose to use to indicate our aesthetic approval, in making that judgment we are applauding the choices made by the writer. As every writer knows, every word in a piece of writing is a choice, a choice which may be easy or difficult, but always a choice to use one word rather than another, one sequence rather than another.

We can fall in love with a person, or a text, in one of two ways. We can fall in love instantaneously, unthinkingly: a text or a person moves us the first time we meet them. Obviously, in order for that to happen, there has to be a powerful correspondence between the chooser and the chosen. Or, we can come to love someone gradually. We can be taught to love them, or we can teach ourselves to do so. We can, over time, get used to their behaviors, become comfortable with them, grow fond of them, until finally we cannot imagine life without them. (Middleton's Bianca, in this way, eventually falls in love with a man who began their relationship by raping her.) In either case, our choice reveals or helps to create a set of correspondences between ourselves and the text, between the choices someone else made and the choices we make.

The more important a text or a person becomes to us, the more important those correspondences of choice are. Because—and this is my ninth observation—

In order to choose, we have to believe in the abiding importance of something above and beyond the particulars of the choice itself. We choose by isolating the differences between our options, and deciding which of those differences is most important, and we can only do that by constructing an explicit or implicit hierarchy of principles, a pyramid of propositions, about the world. Othello murders Desdemona because he believes that sexual fidelity matters more than the life of the woman he loves. Portia acquiesces in the random verdict of the caskets because she believes that filial obedience to the law of the father matters more than a woman's right to choose. DeFlores and Beatrice-Joanna both believe that the satisfaction of their own sexual will matters more than a man's life; this shared belief eventually and naturally leads them to share a bed and then a grave.

Our choices too are governed by propositions of value. When we insist on the inclusion of works by female, non-white, working class, or queer writers, we are acting upon propositions about the importance of gender, race, class, and sexual orientation, about the history of oppression of certain categories of person, about the moral and political imperative for canonical affirmative action, etc. But even when we decide to undo the prejudices of the old canon, we are still forced to make choices which depend on other propositions. In selecting works to include in the new Penguin anthology of Renaissance verse, David Norbrook clearly chose from the outset to diversify the demographical profile of the canon; but he still had to choose how many poems, and which poems, by Aemilia Lanyer or Isabella Whitney or Katherine Philips or Mary Sidney to include. Those choices, like his choices about poems by Donne, Herbert, and all the other educated upper-class males, were governed by propositions about the essential nature of poetry and the essential nature of the world. We have to choose, and we can only choose by being essentialists. We are all essentialists, whether or not we choose to admit the fact.

And we are all guilty, whether or not we choose to admit the fact. Because—and this is my tenth and final observation—

Our choices limit the choices of others. The sixty-four contributors to the Oxford Middleton have made thousands of choices, all based upon debatable propositions about the essential nature of the world. People will quarrel with many of those choices; indeed, they have already begun to do so. They will quarrel, in part, because, for the foreseeable future, there will only be one edition of Middleton's Collected Works in print. The choices all those contributors have made, the choices I have imposed on those contributors, will limit your choices, by affecting the texts available for you to read. But your choices have also been limited by all the other people who have chosen not to edit, not to publish, not to teach Middleton these many years. And our choices about what to edit, what to teach, limit the choices of our students, unavoidably. After all, if we start teaching Middleton, or Lucy Hutchinson, we will not be teaching something else.

We have to choose, even though our choices are limited; but once we have chosen, we limit the choices of others. In choosing or not choosing to read or teach or edit an author's work, we are judging the choices that an author made; and, like those authors, *we* will be judged by the choices *we* make, including—perhaps especially including—the choices we pretend that we are not making at all.

The Children's Middleton

GAIL KERN PASTER

B ECAUSE THE BIBLIOGRAPHIC AND EDITORIAL GAINS OF A NEWLY
collected Middleton are self-evident, I wish to speak here about the
losses, at least as they accrue to one originally anonymous city comedy.
The play in question is *Michaelmas Term*, published in 1607 in a text identified
on its title page as faithful to its performances: "Michaelmas Terme. / AS / IT
HATH BEEN SVN-/dry times acted by the Children of Paules."[1] The losses
in question attend our displacement of the acting children's memorial function
on the title page with that of the author. In retrofitting—even perhaps
retro*flattening*—the oeuvre of so dispersed a writing career as Middleton's
under the romantic rubric of the single, solitary author, an erasure of material
history and local practice occurs. That erasure is particularly damaging, I
would argue, for play-texts like *Michaelmas Term*, which commemorate not
only the small, odd place in theater history occupied by the boys' companies
but also the complex secular culture of that decaying monument of the
seventeenth-century skyline—St. Paul's Cathedral.

The case in our period for material loss through editorial practice has been
argued powerfully by Marion Trousdale, Margreta de Grazia, and Peter
Stallybrass. Rather than repeat, I merely invoke their arguments here.[2] Addi-

---

[1] London, 1607; STC 17890. The "newly collected Middleton" I refer to is the
Oxford Middleton, gen. ed. Gary Taylor, forthcoming.

[2] Marion Trousdale, "A Trip through the Divided Kingdoms," *SQ* 37 (1986):
218–223; and Margreta de Grazia and Peter Stallybrass, "The Materiality of the Shakespearean Text," *SQ* 44 (1993): 255–283.

tionally, however, I wish to argue that the rubric of dramatic authorship, whether applied to Middleton or to Shakespeare, rarely attends to performance; and, when it does so, tends to premise a norm of performance by actors *outside* the City—a norm which signally fails to include the acting children of Paul's.[3] But in the case of *Michaelmas Term*, as for the other plays written for the Children, primary filiations are no less to its actors than to its author, and no less to the meanings of the Cathedral space which the boys briefly occupied.

Indeed, were it not for the fact that so many play-texts from the Children of Paul's survive, the boys' company flourishing briefly at St. Paul's would almost have disappeared from view. Just as the demographic history of Southwark can be—and, in fact, recently has been—written with almost no mention of the public playhouses that loom so large in our differently focused histories,[4] so too the place of the boy actors in the long history of Paul's is much less visible to urban or church historians than it is to historians of sexual and literary culture. Unlike the public playhouses in Southwark, the Cathedral boys' playing space cannot be found in any panoramic view of seventeenth-century London and has not been identified with certainty now. Lost to viewers then in the overshadowing profile of the massive Cathedral, the location of that space remains a matter of archival guesswork and scholarly debate.

But this theater's precise location in the precincts of Paul's does not matter to my argument. What does matter, as Steven Mullaney and others have reminded us, is that the meanings we can attach to *any* given theatrical space in early modern English culture are a function of its immediate historical, topographical, and ideological contexts (Mullaney, 56–57). But the marginality and ambivalent social instrumentality that Mullaney describes for the public playhouses as a result of their move to the outlying liberties cannot be transferred without substantial alteration to the small company of adolescent males engaged in play-making under the questionable aegis of their masters somewhere within the "liberty" of St. Paul's. Just as the specific ideological functions of the public playhouses in the symbolic economy of early modern England derive in part from the local history of Southwark, so too the ideological freightage of the children's plays cannot be divorced without loss from the social history of the Cathedral. The point is not only that, because location signifies, all "liberties" were not the same. It is also that we should question how much the Children of Paul's ought to share in our historical narratives

---

[3] I am thinking of influential works like Steven Mullaney, *The Place of the Stage: License, Play, and Power in Renaissance England* (Chicago: Univ. of Chicago Press, 1988).

[4] Jeremy Boulton, *Neighbourhood and Society: A London Suburb in the Seventeenth Century* (Cambridge: Cambridge Univ. Press, 1987).

about the public playhouses across the water, since they differ in point of origin and date of demise, in authority, in repertory, in price structure for admissions, and, most important for this argument, in immediate social context. However indistinguishable—or not—the *audiences* of the two traditions may have been, to meld the repertories together under the centralizing mantle of the author-function and the precincts of a collected volume is to efface the peculiarly shaping force of the culture of the Cathedral itself. Thus, while Reavley Gair has argued that the plays Middleton wrote for Paul's boys could be performed by any of the adult companies,[5] there is reason to think otherwise. The important work Theodore B. Leinwand has done on the play's persistent sodomitical *double entendres* opens up one discourse in which the materially embodied presence of boy actors matters.[6] I want to follow up and extend Leinwand's work here by framing a more general case for the boys' particularity in order to place the homoerotic dynamics of the play within the larger symbolic and material economy of St. Paul's.

As a theatrical venue, St. Paul's was unlike any other in the period—in the first place, because of its role as the central site of an increasingly powerful print culture. The reader-buyer of *Michaelmas Term* found the quarto for sale within the same precincts where he had seen it performed—and where, by 1607, he could see it no longer. But more important is that, even in a city of highly semiotized spaces, the area within and around the Cathedral may have been the most densely semiotized space of all. It was the locus of a set of highly particularized and powerfully determining secular rituals of time, space, and specularity—rituals that, like the decaying physical fabric of the church itself, seemed to defy all official efforts at stabilization or control.

Historically recoverable meanings for the playing space at the Cathedral, then, depend necessarily on the heterogeneous ensemble of local practices— social, commercial, religious, educational—which had grown up there in a volatile, expansive combination of self-interested profiteering and laissez-faire adhocracy. That the boys had a space in which to perform at the Cathedral at all was a function of local practice in allowing ecclesiastical administrators to lease out space belonging to them *ex officio*; the song-school master garnered theatrical profits because he allowed himself this use of his own space, while the bishop of London and other branches of the ecclesiastical community of Paul's let out areas within the Cathedral precinct, including side chapels within the building itself, to bookbinders, glaziers, stationers, and a variety of other shopkeepers and artisans. An assortment of structures grew up along the

---

[5] *The Children of Paul's: The Story of a Theatre Company 1553–1608* (Cambridge: Cambridge Univ. Press, 1982), 154.

[6] "Redeeming Beggary/Buggary in *Michaelmas Term*," *ELH* 61 (1994): 53–70.

outside of the building, above and below ground level, filling up the church-
yard and shrinking the *cordon sanitaire* of the sacred to the small, walled-off
area of the choir where service was sung.[7] Ethically tendentious historians of
St. Paul's decry the early modern history of the Cathedral as one of physical
and moral encroachment on the space and practices of worship. Or, like John
Stow, on aesthetic grounds they protest compromises to the Cathedral's archi-
tectural integrity: the "south side of S. *Paules* Church, with the chapter
House, (a beautifull peece of worke, builded about the raigne of *Edwarde* the
third) is now defaced by means of Licences graunted to Cutlers, Budget
makers, and other, first to builde low sheddes, but now high Houses, which
doe hide that beautifull side of the Church."[8] A less partisan narrative would
merely note the mutual and thorough interpenetration of city and cathedral,
which was periodically, but futilely, decried by the bishop and dean and by a
succession of monarchs. The Cathedral "is the great exchange of all discourse," wrote Bishop John Earle in 1628, "and no business whatsoever but
is here stirring and afoot."[9] Amid such interpenetration, playing at St. Paul's
was only one in an ensemble of entrepreneurial practices brought into being
and held together by the strong advantage of their common location in a site
the city's social and commercial energies could not resist invading.

What I am imagining, then—not so much symbolized by the Cathedral,
as situated within it—is a form of impersonal, collectivized material intention
in which the song-school plays participate, an intention made legible to us by
the Cathedral's contemporary prominence as a point of physical and discursive
convergence. Francis Osborn noted that "men of all professions not merely
Mechanick ... meet in Paul's Church by eleven, and walk in the middle Ile
till twelve, and after dinner from three to six, during which time some dis-
coursed of Businesse, others of Newes" (quoted in Gair, *The Children of Paul's*,
29). The decaying building and its yard was a semiotically hybrid ground, a
site of physical labor for some and social labor for others; it was a place where
social meanings and commercial enterprises proliferated in an intensely competitive, highly differentiated atmosphere.

The centrality of Paul's becomes a necessary hermeneutic backdrop for
dramatic and satiric appropriations of the site, especially for the city comedies
performed there. Thus the social ritual that for Osborn is a matter of merely
factual information becomes an ethical topos in the more interested narratives

---

[7] For these details, see Gair, 13–43.

[8] *A Survey of London*, ed. Charles Lethbridge Kingsford (Oxford: Clarendon,
1971), 2: 19.

[9] *Microcosmography* (1628), quoted in W. Sparrow Simpson, *Chapters in the History
of Old St. Paul's* (London: Elliot Stock, 1881), 241.

of playwrights like Dekker and Middleton. Dekker's *Gull's Hornbook*, for example, promotes itself ironically as an essential instrument of primary enculturation by likening its own influence in the aspirant reader's life to that of the Cathedral: "Paul's is your Walk, but this your guide."[10] Dekker's satire produces a compelling rhetorical double-bind, reinscribing the behaviors it isolates for ridicule. In it, as in Osborn's comment about "men not merely Mechanick" quoted above, the Cathedral is seen to reproduce and multiply differences by structuring the times for social display and business transactions in an enormous stage-set filled with space-time segmentations far more complex and treacherous than anything actors faced on actual stages. Thus Dekker advises his reader-pupil which part of the Cathedral at which hour of the day is to be selected for self-display, which part is to be shunned:

> Your Mediterranean Aisle is then the only gallery wherein the pictures of all your true fashionate and complimental gulls are and ought to be hung up. Into that gallery carry your neat body. But take heed you pick out such an hour when the main shoal of Aislanders are swimming up and down. And first observe your doors of entrance and exit not much unlike the players at the theatres. (*Dekker*, 88)

Cultivating the skill to read and properly display oneself within the Cathedral's ritualistic space-time becomes part of the gallant's work of achieving maximal specularity. In fact, Dekker makes Paul's interior so thoroughly saturated with semiotic difference that not to know one's place at Paul's was to risk the injury of a potentially shameful misreading by others. He warns of the dangers of being identified with that section of Paul's Walk belonging to servants looking for work:

> [B]e circumspect and wary what pillar you come in at and take heed in any case, as you love the reputation of your honour, that you avoid the Servingman's Log and approach not within five fathom of that pillar but bend your course directly in the middle line, that the whole body of the church may appear to be yours. (*Dekker*, 88–89)

That London literacy and specularity began at Paul's Walk is also posited in the opening scene of *Michaelmas Term*, where a variety of Paul's characters and behaviors converge in a satirically overdetermined social fatality in which distinctions of gender but especially of class are rigorously specularized and evaluated. Richard Easy, the credulous protagonist, is so dispossessed of fundamental Paul's literacy that he has to be told that the notices posted on the

---

[10] *Thomas Dekker*, ed. E. D. Pendry (Cambridge, MA: Harvard Univ. Press, 1968), 69.

pillars of the Middle Aisle are "bills for chambers" (1.1.138) to be let.[11]
More crucially, while he seems capable of recognizing the stigmatized specularity of others like the Scottish arriviste Andrew Lethe, he is shown to be
vulnerable to the intrigue mounted against him precisely because he is ignorant of his own specularity: "A fair free-breasted gentleman, somewhat too
open," the gallant Cockstone remarks disparagingly, who "wants the city
powd'ring" (1.1.53, 56). That Easy should arrive at Paul's virtually at the same
moment as Ephestian Quomodo, the man who would dispossess him, trans-
forms narrative coincidence into an urban purposiveness endemic to Paul's
Walk (it was, after all, where Falstaff hired Bardolph). "That's he, that's he,"
Quomodo exclaims to his shape-shifting assistant Shortyard, "Observe, take
surely note of him, he's fresh and free" (1.1.119, 121). The potential injury of
the gaze is not peculiar to Easy's situation, however: the gallant Rearage
shrinks from the view of Quomodo; Andrew Lethe compulsively seeks out
the role of cynosure hoping to attract the attention of a "necessary bawd"
(238), only to find that his desire for specularity brings him the unwanted
notice of his abandoned mother. He is spared the shame of this social mis-
recognition by his own difference from himself: "Good, she knows me not,"
he exclaims in relief, "my glory does disguise me" (271). Later, a similar transformation through clothes in the Country Wench will prevent her father from
recognizing her.

The opening scene in *Michaelmas Term* seems dedicated to demonstrating
the dense proliferation of meanings and encounters in Paul's as an engine of
massive social dislocation in London. The transformations that prevent parents
from recognizing their sartorially—hence socially—altered children work to
disrupt the social mirrorings which, in theory, allowed everyone to find his
own social place through fixed difference with that of others. But the semiotic
confusions endemic to the Cathedral's space-time complexity produce a pro-
liferating set of social mirrors that disperse images, confounding rather than
enabling social self-construction. Dekker thus describes the "true humorous
gallant that desires to pour himself into all fashions ... to excel even
compliment itself" (*Dekker*, 88).

In *Michaelmas Term*, as in *The Gull's Hornbook*, relentless specularity is the
enforcer of lack, hence the ground of all erotics—whether homoerotics or the
erotics of class mobility. In the play, this specularity, while it is not narratively
caused by Paul's Walk, is significantly sited there. In the midst of this semiotic

---

[11] I quote here from the most accessible modern edition of the play in "*A Mad
World, My Masters*" and Other Plays, ed. Michael Taylor (Oxford: Oxford Univ. Press,
1995). Two editions of the play, mine for the Revels Plays and Theodore Leinwand's
for the Oxford Middleton, are forthcoming.

welter, the choristers were at one and the same time the exploited, the exploiters, and the collaborators. They were subjects and objects of intense specularity in a complex of roles. Even their customary privilege of collecting spur-money from whoever entered the Cathedral wearing prohibited spurs, for example, required a combination of locally advantageous traits—aggressiveness, ubiquitousness, sharp eyes, imperfect absorption in the singing of service, the ability simultaneously to play several roles, and the ability to attract socially requisite attention in a highly competitive specular economy. Thus Dekker advises his gallant to attach himself to the boys' specularity:

> [B]e sure your silver spurs dog your heels, and then the boys will swarm about you like so many white butterflies when you in the open Choir shall draw forth a perfumed embroidered purse—the glorious sight of which will entice many countrymen from their devotion, to wondering; and quoit silver into the boys' hands that it may be heard above the first lesson, although it be read in a voice as big as one of the great organs. (*Dekker*, 90)

Onstage and off, it is cultivation of proximity to the proliferation of meanings and meaningful encounters at Paul's that structures the boys' cultural function—not, as in the case of the players outside the city, the ideologically strategic calculation of distance. It is a cultural function that Middleton does not invent for the boys, but one that he powerfully exploits in *Michaelmas Term* and in the other city comedies written for them. It is the boys' proximity which makes the metatheatricality and homoerotic *double entendres* pervading *Michaelmas Term* almost a structural inevitability. For the "homosocial circuit" into which the character Easy wishes to insinuate himself by coming up to London—I am paraphrasing Leinwand here (57)—in the play is one in which the children of Paul's moved everyday, whether they were the choirboys who swarmed like white butterflies around the gallants in spurs or those who took the stage late in the afternoon when the "men not merely Mechanick" would return after dinner to the Cathedral precincts and perhaps take in a play.

Far more than authorship categories, then, it is the powerful symbolic economy of St. Paul's Cathedral that ought to ground our historical narratives about the children's plays. In this economy theater-going was one in a complex of *locally* specific practices dependent for their social and material potency on the Cathedral's agreed-upon centrality in early modern London. Because the theater and the acting boys of Paul's form a narrative of their own, our insertion of them into narratives centered on authorship or on the ideological functions of other theatrical venues flattens a material landscape of theatrical differentiation into one looking all too much the same.

"The Lady Vanishes": Problems of Authorship and Editing in the Middleton Canon

JULIA BRIGGS

THE TUNNEL VISION ASSOCIATED WITH CANONICITY HAS LONG been recognized as a deformity that criticism must continually interrogate, but it has proved particularly intractable in the case of Renaissance drama, where play-texts have survived in reasonable numbers, but only a strictly limited group are regularly re-read, reprinted or, more crucially, performed, even though they were written primarily for performance, and without it, their main artistic raison d'être has been lost. Nineteenth-century editors, men such as W. C. Hazlitt, Alexander Dyce, and the ill-fated Churton Collins, made strenuous efforts to collect and reprint Renaissance play-texts, and comparably strenuous efforts were made to stage them by Edward Craig, William Poel, and the Phoenix Society (whose productions crucially influenced T. S. Eliot's criticism). In England, this tradition is maintained by the Royal Shakespeare Company, which recently performed such neglected plays as Heywood's *The Fair Maid of the West*, and *A Woman Killed with Kindness*, and Brome's *Jovial Crew* (though in the last instance, the director lost confidence in the existing text and incorporated a radical rewriting).

The problems of canonicity are inseparable from the cult of the author: for performance and reproduction, there is an established order of priority, with Shakespeare and Jonson, whose works were collected in folio, at the base of a putative pyramid; on the other hand, the Beaumont and Fletcher (or, more correctly, Massinger and Fletcher) collaboration includes more plays than can easily be remembered, and so has been neglected. After Jonson follow the small-oeuvre playwrights, Marlowe and the non-collaborative tragedies of Webster, but collaborative plays, even when they are as good as *Eastward Ho!* are either seldom performed, or else are effectively attributed to the better-known of their authors (as the treatment of *The Changeling* indicates). Anonymous plays later than the mystery cycles fare worst of all, languishing unreprinted and almost never performed.

Middleton's reputation has suffered from these arbitrary processes of selection largely because his works were not collected until the nineteenth century, even though they were clearly popular both during and after his life time: the King's Men actively maintained their rights in them, and they were extensively plundered by Restoration playwrights. Today, two or three of his comedies are regularly included in collections of city comedies, while *The Changeling* and *Women Beware Women* appear in most anthologies of revenge tragedy. *Hengist, King of Kent*, dealing with subjects as topical as nationhood, power and sexual exploitation, is never reprinted, seldom taught or discussed, and only very rarely performed, and the tragi-comedies are similarly neglected. In Middleton's case, even the concept of authorship seems to have worked as Barthes and Foucault warned that it did—only to pre-determine an exclusive view of the kind of writer he was. Thus the attribution to Middleton of *The Revenger's Tragedy* has been dismissed on the grounds that the tragedies were composed late in his career (despite the missing *Chester Tragedy,* for which Philip Henslowe paid him in 1602, and *The Viper and Her Brood*, referred to in a lawsuit of 1606); or, starting from the opposite end of the argument, that the stereotyped characters of *The Revenger's Tragedy* are too different from the psychological studies of the late tragedies to be the work of the same author. Attempts at new attributions have thus occasioned limiting assumptions that set artificial boundaries on Middleton's development, even though a possible progress from *The Revenger's Tragedy* to the later plays is precisely what is at stake.

This reductive concept of authorship has operated to isolate *The Revenger's Tragedy,* along with the rest of the Middleton apocrypha, and has arguably worked to reduce its appearance in taught courses and on the stage; at the same time, identifiable authorship is still the concept most frequently used in the study of Renaissance drama to confer meaning and shape interpretation, as well as to guarantee and authenticate publication and performance. To attribute *The Revenger's Tragedy* to Middleton is thus to set it in a familiar literary landscape, an existing and identifiable body of work which yields relevant analogies: these might include symbolically named characters such as those of *The Phoenix* (notably Lussurioso and Castiza), the sense of social indignation to be found in pamphlets such as *The Ant and the Nightingale* and *The Black Book* ("that smooth glittering devil, satin, and that old reveller velvet ... have devoured many an honest field of wheat and barley"; Bullen, 16), and a wider political sensibility that found its ultimate expression in *A Game at Chess*. The concept of an author can confer meaning as effectively as it can constrict it.

While an exclusive concern with authorship has undermined the proper appreciation of many collaborative or anonymous Renaissance plays, attribution can provide a rich source of new meanings: once an author's canon is reconstructed and an individual play takes its place among a sequence of others, its characteristics become apparent within the network of new relationships. And however properly skeptical we may be about the concept of the author, any play's linguistic relationship to a wider corpus is always significantly closer to and more familial with other plays by that author than with contemporary plays of different authorship. While particular discourses and cultural signifiers help to shape the play-texts of a given year or a given genre, individual turns of phrase, usage and writing practices are as unique and unmistakable as fingerprints. Thus while the anonymous *Second Maiden's Tragedy* (late 1611) has unexpected affinities with Shakespeare's *Winter's Tale* (May, 1611), with Webster's *White Devil* (early 1612) and *The Duchess of Malfi* (1613–1614), and Tourneur's *The Atheist's Tragedy* (1611), it has much closer linguistic links with the Middleton-Dekker collaboration *The Roaring Girl*, and Middleton's *No Wit, No Help Like a Woman's* (both 1611), city comedies that, while unrelated in subject matter, yet yield remarkable verbal parallels.

Part of the pleasure in editing *The Second Maiden's Tragedy* for the Oxford *Complete Works of Thomas Middleton* lies in rescuing it from the oblivion that anonymity perpetuates. Its attribution to Middleton was first tentatively proposed by Swinburne more than a century ago, and then more confidently asserted by Oliphant, Barker, Schoenbaum, and Holdsworth, and confirmed by the linguistic tests applied by David Lake and MacDonald P. Jackson in the 1970s. In an excellent Revels edition of the play, Anne Lancashire set out the evidence for Middleton's authorship, including the relevant linguistic parallels, but she could not finally bring herself to publish Middleton's name on the title page, even though all the evidence seemed to point to that conclusion. Lake and Jackson in particular have been closely involved in reuniting the dismembered fragments of the Middleton canon, though *The Complete Works* will go substantially further than they have done by including neglected prose such as *Plato's Cap* and *The Owl's Almanac*, as well as *Timon of Athens*, *Macbeth* and, more surprisingly, *Measure for Measure*.

It is a rewarding experience to welcome *The Second Maiden's Tragedy* back into circulation at a moment when its magnificent heroine should receive the recognition that is her due, but the play survives only in a single manuscript that itself presents further challenges to the concept of authorship, since it records extensive revision by different hands that may or may not be authorized. While the evidence does not point conclusively to any consistent line of development, processes of censorship re-direct the text away from its earliest state, and many further cuts, additions, and alterations have been made, whose authority must remain in doubt. The difficulty of deciding exactly what kind of processes are at work may be represented by the problem of the missing title page. Its loss would explain the play's anonymity and the clumsy provisional title conferred on the play by Sir George Buc, master of the Revels and the licenser. Such a loss might be read as anticipating the series of developments, each of which takes the manuscript a significant step further from its point of origin, beginning with the loss of title and author, determining factors in the subsequent history of any Renaissance play. But the loss of the title page is itself a matter of conjecture. There is no evidence for or against its existence: the manuscript may either have had one and lost it before it was submitted to Buc at the Revels Office, or may never have had one at all. The manuscript of *The Second Maiden's Tragedy* is now in the British Library (Lansdowne 807). Complete manuscripts of plays are comparatively unusual: Shakespeare and Jonson's plays survive mainly in the form of printed texts, though there are manuscript versions of Jonson's masques, and some leaves from the manuscript of *Sir Thomas More* appear to be in Shakespeare's hand. There are several surviving manuscripts of Middleton's plays, though these are typically in the form of presentation copies, decoratively set out and folded into quartos so that they may be conveniently sent and read: *The Witch* in a transcript by the King's Men's scribe, Ralph Crane; *Hengist, King of Kent* in two closely related later manuscripts, and six manuscripts of *A Game at Chess*, the Trinity copy in Middleton's own hand and three made by Ralph Crane. The manuscript of *The Second Maiden's Tragedy* uses the full folio page. It is clearly written out in an elegant secretary hand that is neither Crane's nor Middleton's, though it belongs to a professional scribe employed, as Crane was, by the King's Men. It has been used as a promptbook. According to Greg, there are sixteen promptbooks of plays written for the public theatre before 1640, and of these sixteen, a quarter have been subjected to censorship by Buc as Master of the Revels from 1603 to 1622: these are *Woodstock* (or *1 Richard II*), *Charlemagne*, Fletcher and Massinger's *Sir John Van Olden Barnavelt* and *The Second Maiden's Tragedy* (T. H. Howard-Hill, "Marginal Markings," 168–170). This manuscript has been substantially corrected by Buc on behalf of the Revels Office. He is responsible for the deletion of sixteen oaths ("Heart!" five times; "Life!" ten times; and one "By the mass!") and a reference to the horrible death of François Ravaillac, the fanatic who had assassinated Henry IV in the previous year ("beyond the Frenchmen's tortures," at 5.2.140). He also deleted a number of adverse references to the court and courtiers:

> ... heaven, / That glorious court of spirits, all honest courtiers!
> (last three words deleted; 1.2.14–15)

> ... I must put on / A courtier's face and do't. Mine own will
>   shame me.
> ("courtier's" deleted; "brazen" substituted: 1.2.164–165)

> Push, talk like a courtier, girl, not like a fool.
> ("courtier" deleted; "woman" substituted: 2.1.69)

> There's many a good knight's daughter is in service
> And cannot get such favour of her mistress ...
> ("knight's" deleted; "men's" substituted: 4.1.74)

> I would not trust at court, an I could choose.
> ("at court" deleted; "but few" substituted: 5.2.80)

Buc also marked for removal a number of passages commenting specifically on the behaviour of court ladies:

> Thou know'st the end of greatness, and hast wit
> Above the flight of twenty feathered mistresses
> That glister in the sun of princes' favours. (2.1.70–72)

And in the following lines, "most" has been replaced by "many":

> Nothing hurt thee but want of woman's counsel:
> Hadst thou but asked th'opinion of most ladies,
> Thou'dst never come to this! (4.3.101–103)

The play's final couplet is similarly muted by the substitution of "virtuous" for "honest" (the latter had strong sexual connotations), but the change spoils the meter and undermines the echo of "honours" in the previous line:

> I would those ladies that fill honour's rooms
> Might all be borne so honest to their tombs. (5.2 211–212)

Underneath this couplet, on the final page, Buc added:

This second Maydens tragedy (for it hath no name inscribed) may w[i]th the reformations bee acted publikely. 31 octob[e]r 1611. By me G. Buc.

Thus it was Buc who gave the play not only a date, but also the title by which it came to be known. This provisional title resulted from the play's pointed criticism of the court, which recalled that of Beaumont's *Maid's Tragedy*, submitted for his approval in the previous year. But this is unlikely to have been the title under which it was performed since maidens and maidenhoods, as such, scarcely figure in this text at all, whereas they are a notable feature of Beaumont's *Maid's Tragedy* ("A maidenhead, Amintor, / At my years?"). Ladies, on the other hand, provide a frequent point of reference: the play's heroine is the unnamed Lady (Middleton's avoidance of names here, and in the case of the Tyrant, is in marked contrast to the characterizing names given earlier in *The Revenger's Tragedy*—a development that Anne Barton has observed independently [78–81]), and the central character of the sub-plot is referred to four times in the original stage directions as "Anselmus' Lady." There are also the several references to the misbehavior of court ladies whose presence Buc sought to reduce. Since Middleton had earlier used the title *The Revenger's* (or *Revengers'*) *Tragedy*, this play is likely to have been *The Lady's* or *Ladies' Tragedy*.

Back at the playhouse, the manuscript underwent a further round of cuts and substitutions. A number of small changes were made by unidentified hands, some apparently with the intention of tidying the meter, others for no very obvious reason at all (e.g., "way" changed to "path" at 2.1.158; "limber" changed to "fearful" at 4.3.28; "fate's my hindrance" to "fate is my hinderer" at 5.2.32). At points in the manuscript, circles were drawn in the margin and five addition slips were pasted in, all of them cut from a single folio page and written out by the scribe who had copied the manuscript. In general the additions serve to expand or elucidate inconsistencies in the plot, but the penultimate one covers an exit and immediate re-entry by the Tyrant at a different location (between 4.2 and 4.3), while the last provides a small but unforgettable peripeteia. In the original version, Anselmus, whose distrust has destroyed his marriage, dies wrongly believing that his wife had remained faithful to him throughout: "I thank thee, fate. / I expire cheerfully and give death a smile" (5.1.141–142). In the revision, he survives long enough to discover that he has been deceived and dies, repenting "the smile / That I bestowed on destiny" and pronouncing a last misogynistic couplet:

> O thou beguiler of man's easy trust,
> The serpent's wisdom is in woman's lust!

Yet even with these additions, the play was still not ready for the stage: further cuts were now made, especially to the last scene, whose length was substantially reduced, probably to allow sufficient time for the two contrasting ceremonies of homage to the Lady's corpse: the idolatrous worship of the Tyrant and her formal coronation by Govianus. One character's part, that of

Helvetius, was entirely deleted from this scene. These cuts must have been made after the addition slips were composed, since the penultimate slip describes Helvetius as about to be released by the conspirators against the Tyrant, thus explaining his presence in the final scene. The manuscript was finally marked up by the book holder who wrote further stage directions in the margin in an italic hand, calling for sound effects such as sennets, flourishes, and in the *Macbeth*-inspired act 3, frequent off-stage knocking. And in the process of reminding himself of all these cues, he provided further details: in act 4, against the additional speech covering the Tyrant's re-entry he wrote "Enter Mr / Goughe," and at the entry of the Lady's Ghost at 4.4.42 he wrote "Enter Ladye / Rich Robinson," thus proving decisively that the play was acted by the King's Men, and in all probability performed at the Blackfriars Theatre one afternoon early in the winter of 1611. To read the manuscript is thus to feel oneself in the presence of the playhouse scrivener and book holder, as Jonson was to present them in the prologue to *Bartholomew Fair*, more than two years later. But whether Middleton remained the puppet-master, controlling their pens, or whether he had withdrawn is impossible to judge.

While his contribution to the play's revisions and rehearsals remains a matter for conjecture, his detectable presence is most evident in the earliest state of the manuscript which records a number of spellings and forms characteristic of his practice in the Trinity College holograph of *A Game at Chess* and to some extent preserved in the quartos, including, MacDonald Jackson has argued, that of *The Revenger's Tragedy*. These include Middleton's notorious use of oaths—"life," "heart," "cuds me," "push" (the first two extensively deleted by Buc), his frequent use of elisions of various kinds, a number of eccentric spellings (notably a "-cst" suffix—"forcst" (1.2.91; 3.1.97; "placst," "gracst" 4.4.14, 16), and the idiosyncratic placing of apostrophes and deployment of punctuation marks—exclamation marks, question marks and a form of reversed question mark which Malcolm Parkes classifies as "punctus percontativus," associated (though not always consistently in the manuscript) with rhetorical questions.

Judged on the basis of vocabulary and style, the additional slips are also the work of Middleton (though Eric Rasmussen has argued for Shakespeare's hand in them). If this is the case, the manuscript revisions include authorial intervention, although the subsequent cutting of Helvetius's part from the final scene may or may not have been made with his agreement. There is an intriguing parallel here with *Hengist, King of Kent* where, in the play's final moments, Castiza's part, as it appears in the two manuscript versions, has been entirely cut from the quarto text (itself supposed to derive from a promptbook, while the manuscripts are thought to represent earlier states of the text).

Grace Ioppolo has recently argued that the alteration, rather than occurring in the playhouse, is one of several authorial revisions that significantly alter the balance of the play. If the cutting of Helvetius's part were also to be regarded as part of a process of authorial revision, it might simplify the dilemma that confronts the editor of this manuscript.

Graphically, in every sense, the manuscript records a series of different stages of development, from an initial authorial conception as set out in the scribe's fair copy, through a series of deletions made at the Revels Office and insertions, substitutions, and further deletions made at the playhouse, until it reaches the latest version, presumably as performed by the King's Men's at the Blackfriars. Working from the manuscript, an editor could provide the text as performed, incorporating the various cuts and changes it had undergone. While its original political bite has been significantly muzzled, this was the form in which it was known to Middleton's contemporaries (who immediately began to borrow from it, as the pistol shots at the end of *The White Devil* and the whole conception of *The Duchess of Malfi* demonstrate). This, too, is the form it would have taken had it ever been printed—as a play that had been through the process of adaptation for performance. To reproduce the earliest state, by contrast, is to reproduce a play that never was, a text that only the author, the scribe and possibly Sir George Buc would have recognized, a textual cul-de-sac, for the sake of that deeply dubious concept, the author's original intention.

The issue is an interesting one because it recapitulates a fundamental split in editing principles between the now outmoded idea of reconstituting the text closest to its point of origin (and, probably, to the author in this case) and more recent interest in the process by which a play-text passes from the private into the public domain. In the end it was decided to include both the earliest (and most politically radical) version, alongside the version of the play that was finally performed, as a vivid illustration of just what changes a text might undergo in the playhouse.

The manuscript's after-life was not uneventful: it surfaced briefly in an entry in the Stationers' Register for 9 September 1653, when the printer Humphrey Moseley entered some forty or so plays for publication, including *The History of Cardenio* by Mr Fletcher and Shakespeare, and a group of Middleton plays that includes *More Dissemblers Besides Women, Women Beware Women, No Wit, No Help Like a Woman's* and *The Puritan*, a list that has been of importance in reconstructing the Middleton canon and that reflects Moseley's possession of a significant number of play-texts performed by the King's Men. There follows a list of Massinger plays, and then an entry for "The Maid's Tragedie, 2d part," which suggests that the manuscript was now in Moseley's hands and was already identified only by Buc's provisional title on the final page. Incidentally, the entry as a whole establishes that *The Second Maiden's Tragedy* is not identical with the *History of Cardenio* as Charles Hamilton's recent edition of it argues, or, at any rate, that Moseley thought them sufficiently distinct to make separate entries for them in the Register.

If Moseley possessed the manuscript, he never published it, and the first recorded owner was John Warburton, nearly a century later. It has been argued that Warburton acquired Moseley's stock since the list of the plays once in his possession corresponds closely to Moseley's list entered in the Stationers' Register for 9 September 1653 and at a later entry, for 29 June 1660. According to Warburton, the manuscript narrowly escaped a culinary demise, when his collection of plays was destroyed through the carelessness of his servant, being "unluckily burned or put under pie bottoms, excepting the 3 which follow," the other two that escaped being *The Bugbears* (1564) and *The Queen of Corsica* (1642). After Warburton's death his collection was sold, passing through the library of the Marquis of Lansdowne and reaching the British Library in 1807. *The Second Maiden's Tragedy* was published four times in the nineteenth century, first in 1824, twice in 1875 and again in 1892, the last two editions attributing the play to George Chapman, whose name had been written on the final page by a later hand, along with that of Will Shakspear (predictably) and Thomas Goff (presumably because the actor Robert Goughe had been named in the text). So far there have been three twentieth-century editions published: Greg's diplomatic transcript for the Malone Society in 1911, Anne Lancashire's modern-spelling edition, with a full scholarly apparatus, for Revels of 1978, and Charles Hamilton's edition of 1994 which identifies it with the lost play of *Cardenio*. Its fourth appearance will be in the *Complete Works of Middleton*.

The play's long neglect in the twentieth century has not been entirely due to its lack of a positive attribution. In *Middleton's Tragedies* (1955), Samuel Schoenbaum accepted the play as Middleton's, and discussed it at some length, while considering it disappointing: "it has not aroused much enthusiasm" (66), and, as Schelling observed, "[it] is wanting in true dramatic force" (67). He underestimates Swinburne's admiration for it (66) and complains that "It lacks unity of action, the two stories being joined together in a clumsy and arbitrary fashion. Furthermore the main plot is less interesting than the underplot . . ." (37). Schoenbaum is uninterested in the heroic Lady but over-excited by the Wife ("at heart fiercely sensual," 46), and he is reluctant to take the Tyrant's oppression seriously, or to see how carefully his abuse of political power is echoed in Anselmus's abuse of domestic power. His limitations reflect those of a particular moment in critical history, a moment before either politics or gender, let alone the close connections between them, had become central issues in Renaissance drama. For Schoenbaum, the struggle for sexual and political power that drives the plot forward is "unconvincing" and "uninteresting" (58), and Middleton's refusal to limit the application of his story by naming its protagonists is merely another weakness. For Schoenbaum, Middleton the realist had been misled by the popularity of Beaumont and Fletcher into writing a play ill-suited to his talents. Forty years further on, the discovery of an exemplary Middleton heroine, whose courage and love enable her to resist the patriarchal oppression both of her father and of the Tyrant (as head of the state) is wholly welcome. *The Lady's Tragedy* will be eagerly assimilated into the canon where its influence on Middleton's contemporaries, and particularly on Webster, can be properly acknowledged. For Middleton (as for Munday in *The Death of Robert Earl of Huntingdon*, Dekker in *The Virgin Martyr*, and possibly also in *Measure for Measure*), feminine resistance to sexual oppression is not merely heroic in itself, but figures the resistance of the individual subject to state-imposed religion, the defense of chastity paralleling the insistence on individual liberty of conscience. The play's two plots of tested love, so clumsily aligned for Schoenbaum, together exemplify Mary Beth Rose's analysis of the Jacobean "heroics of marriage," which she defines as "embodied in the female protagonist[s] and associated with the future. Yet the heroics of marriage breaks down from external opposition and from internal contradictions that center on conflicting imperatives of gender, power, and social class" (9). She stands up as a woman against a male order that shows no respect for her integrity or self-determination, and her true affinities are with the boisterous but ultimately high-minded Moll Cutpurse, *The Roaring Girl*, or with courageous and ingenious Kate Lowater (*No Wit, No Help Like a Woman's*). "The masterly daring of the stage effect ... is not more characteristic of the author than the tender and passionate fluency of the flawless verse. ... [It] must by all evidence of internal and external probability be almost unquestionably assigned to the hand of Middleton" wrote Swinburne of *The Second Maiden's Tragedy* in 1908. At that time, the obstacle to his intuition was the generally accepted attribution of *The Revenger's Tragedy* to Cyril Tourneur. Now that obstacle has been finally removed, and part of the pleasure in restoring both plays to the Middleton canon is the discovery of their relationships within it: *The Revenger's Tragedy* sits among the early satirical comedies like *Romeo and Juliet* among Shakespeare's "happy" comedies, while *The Lady's Tragedy* provides the missing link between the different tragic modes, combining the political cynicism and harsh laughter of the earlier tragedy (and later of *A Game at Chess*) with the painful domestic insights of *The Changeling*, while introducing a heroine of moral beauty and power. In future we shall be able to teach Middleton's tragedies as a coherent and developing sequence from *The Revenger's* through *The Lady's Tragedy* to *Hengist*, *The Changeling* and *Women Beware Women*. The pivotal position of

The Lady's Tragedy must make us especially glad that, somewhat against the odds, as Warburton described them, it survived fire-lighting and pie-lining. But its long neglect begs troubling questions about the gardens of literature and the other literary wallflowers that languish in them.

Works Cited

Barker, Richard. "The Authorship of the *Second Maiden's Tragedy* and *The Revenger's Tragedy*." *The Shakespeare Association Bulletin* 20 (1945): 52–62, 121–133.

Barton, Anne. *The Names of Comedy*. Oxford: Oxford Univ. Press, 1990.

Holdsworth, R. V., ed. *Three Jacobean Revenge Tragedies: A Casebook*. London: Macmillan, 1990.

Howard-Hill, T. H. "Marginal Markings: The Censor and the Editing of Four English Promptbooks." *Studies in Bibliography* 36 (1983): 168–177.

Ioppolo, Grace. "Revision, Manuscript Transmission and Scribal Practice in Middleton's *Hengist, King of Kent, or, The Mayor of Queenborough*." *Critical Survey* 7.3 (1995): 319–331.

Jackson, MacDonald P. *Studies in Attribution: Middleton and Shakespeare*. Salzburg: Institut für Anglistik und Amerikanistik, 1979.

Lake, David. *The Canon of Thomas Middleton's Plays*. London: Cambridge Univ. Press, 1975.

Middleton, Thomas. *The Works of Thomas Middleton*, ed. A. H. Bullen. 8 vols. London: John C. Nimmo, 1885. Vol. 8 (*The Black Book, Father Hubburd's Tale*, etc.).

———. *A Game at Chess*, ed. T. H. Howard-Hill. London: Malone Society Reprints, 1990.

———. *Hengist, King of Kent; or the Mayor of Queenborough*, ed. R. C. Bald. New York and London: Charles Scribner's Sons, 1938.

———. *The Revenger's Tragedy: a Facsimile of the 1607/8 Quarto*, introduced by MacDonald P. Jackson. London and Toronto: Associated Univ. Presses, 1983.

———. *The Second Maiden's Tragedy*, ed. W. W. Greg. Oxford: Malone Society Reprints, 1909.

———. *The Second Maiden's Tragedy*, ed. Anne Lancashire. Manchester: Manchester Univ. Press; Baltimore: Johns Hopkins Univ. Press, 1978.

Oliphant, E. H. C. "The Authorship of *The Revenger's Tragedy.*" *Studies in Philology* 23 (1926): 157–168.

Parkes, Malcolm. *Pause and Effect: An Introduction to the History of Punctuation in the West.* Aldershot: Scolar Press, 1992.

Rasmussen, Eric. "Shakespeare's Hand in *The Second Maiden's Tragedy.*" *Shakespeare Quarterly* 40 (1989): 1–26.

Rose, Mary Beth. *The Expense of Spirit: Love and Sexuality in English Renaissance Drama.* Ithaca and London: Cornell Univ. Press, 1988.

Schoenbaum, Samuel. *Middleton's Tragedies: A Critical Study.* New York: Columbia Univ. Press, 1955.

Shakespeare, William, and John Fletcher. *The Lost Play of Cardenio or The Second Maiden's Tragedy*, ed. Charles Hamilton. Lakewood, CO: Glenbridge, 1994.

Swinburne, A. C. "Thomas Middleton." *The Age of Shakespeare.* London: Chatto and Windus, 1908.

Editing All the Manuscripts of All The Canterbury Tales *into Electronic Form: Is the Effort Worthwhile?*

ELIZABETH SOLOPOVA

NYONE READING CHAUCER'S *THE HOUSE OF FAME* FOR THE
first time experiences confusion and bewilderment trying to absorb the first paragraphs, which contain a brilliantly condensed and
ambiguous introduction to the medieval theory of dreams.[1] The types,
effects, and causes of dreams are summarized in one long breathless sentence
which comprises about fifty lines of verse. At the end of this exposition the
reader is completely overwhelmed by terms and ideas. I once went to a seminar where a teacher explained the meaning of every word in this catalogue of
dreams specifying what exactly were *somnium, vision, revelation, phantom, swe-
ven, oracle* and so on, as understood and used by Chaucer. Though the theory
of dreams is undoubtedly a useful subject for a scholar of literature, in this
particular context it becomes ironic: anyone taking it seriously will be missing
the point. Chaucer's exposition of dream theory aims not to elucidate, but to
confuse and disorient. His presentation overwhelms the mind and suggests that

---

[1] This paper describes the experience of work of the *Canterbury Tales* Project on
the production of electronic scholarly editions and gives an outline of Peter Robinson's and my research on the textual tradition of the *Tales*. This paper is much indebted to Peter Robinson for collaboration in its preparation and in research here
summarized.

the subject itself is confusing. Such presentation is artfully aimed to suggest an inability to think and to guide. It has been observed in connection with this passage from *The House of Fame* that too much information can be as bad as too little.[2] Information in overwhelming abundance paralyses the mental process instead of stimulating it. These considerations deserve to be taken seriously by editors of electronic texts. The first *Canterbury Tales* Project CD-ROM presents readers accustomed to a single canonical text with at least 117 texts of Chaucer's The Wife of Bath's Prologue: the transcripts of each of the fifty-eight manuscripts, the images of each of these, and the "base text" we use for collation.[3] Is such a publication going to be a valuable resource for reading, studying, and understanding Chaucer, an efficient tool for research, or is it a labyrinth no one wants to enter?

From the very start *The Canterbury Tales* Project electronic publications were intended as scholarly editions, and research tools for investigating the textual tradition of *The Canterbury Tales*. The inspiration for this work and our most important aim is to establish, as nearly as we can, the text of Chaucer's major poem, composed six hundred years ago and received by us in a distorted and imperfect form. As is well known, Chaucer left his text unfinished, and the surviving manuscripts present a picture of considerable textual disorder. The texts of the tales vary from manuscript to manuscript, often markedly; the order of the tales is also unstable. There is no consensus among scholars as to the choice of the best manuscript as the base for an edition. In particular, scholars disagree as to which the two of the most important manuscripts—Hengwrt or Ellesmere—should be used as the basis for a text of *The Canterbury Tales*.[4]

The complexity of the task of investigating the evolution of Chaucer's text

---

[2] S. Delany, *Chaucer's House of Fame: The Poetics of Skeptical Fideism* (Chicago: Univ. of Chicago Press, 1972), 41.

[3] P. M. W. Robinson, ed., *The Wife of Bath's Prologue on CD-ROM,* with contributions from Norman Blake, Daniel W. Mosser, Stephen Partridge and Elizabeth Solopova (Cambridge: Cambridge Univ. Press, 1996).

[4] Aberystwyth, National Library of Wales, Peniarth 392 (the "Hengwrt manuscript") and San Marino, Huntington Library, MS 26.C.9 (the "Ellesmere manuscript"). For information on the Hengwrt–Ellesmere debate see P. G. Ruggiers, ed., *Editing Chaucer: The Great Tradition* (Norman, OK: Pilgrim Books, 1984); N. F. Blake, "The Relationship between the Hengwrt and the Ellesmere Manuscripts of the *Canterbury Tales,*" *Essays and Studies* n.s. 32 (1979), 1–8; "The Ellesmere Text in the Light of the Hengwrt Manuscript" in M. Stevens and D. Woodward, eds., *The Ellesmere Chaucer: Essays in Interpretation* (San Marino, CA: Huntington Library, and Tokyo: Yoshodo Co., 1995), 205–224; R. Hanna, III, "(The) Editing (of) the Ellesmere Text," in the same volume, 225–243.

made us aware of the need for extensive and powerful resources. The failure of earlier scholars, particularly John Manly and Edith Rickert, to complete the study of the textual tradition of the *Tales* was largely due to the inability of manual collation to cope with the multilateral comparison of about ninety widely different manuscripts.[5] We knew that our only chance of succeeding and advancing our purpose within a reasonable time scale was to use quick and efficient methods of computer analysis. What we needed was sophisticated software for collation and comparison of readings, as well as machine-readable and searchable texts in the original spelling.

We decided from the start that we needed to transcribe all the surviving fifteenth-century manuscripts and printed editions. The case with *The Canterbury Tales* is that some of the late and generally unreliable witnesses preserve some very good readings, which became the basis for some of the best-known emendations.[6] So far no one has been able to explain how and why this could have happened. The status of some of the witnesses is not clearly understood: they possibly contain information which will help to resolve the problems we are investigating. One also has to anticipate that estimation of the textual value of manuscripts changes as the work progresses. The manuscript used as the basis for some nineteenth-century editions of the *Tales*— London, British Library, MS Harley 7334—is now believed to contain, in spite of its early date, a heavily edited text many stages removed from the original.[7] Our own view as to which manuscripts are important for establishing Chaucer's text changed dramatically several times in the course of our work. Thus Caxton's second edition of the *Tales,* thought by Manly and Rickert to be of no textual authority and unworthy of being included in their Corpus of Variants and originally included by us in the list of witnesses to be transcribed mostly for the sake of consistency, now plays a very prominent role in our discussion of the textual tradition.[8] Caxton corrected the text for his second edition of the *Tales* from a now lost manuscript, close to Chaucer's

---

[5] J. M. Manly and E. Rickert, eds., *The Text of the Canterbury Tales*, 8 vols. (Chicago: Univ. of Chicago Press, 1940).

[6] For example, E. T. Donaldson's emendation in line 117 of the Wife of Bath's Prologue; see "Chaucer, *Canterbury Tales,* D 117: A Critical Edition," *Speculum* 40 (1965): 626–633.

[7] J. S. P. Tatlock, *The Harleian Manuscript and Revision of the Canterbury Tales* (Chaucer Society, 2nd ser., 41; London: Kegan Paul, Trench, Trubner, 1909).

[8] Manly and Rickert, *The Text of the Canterbury Tales*, 1: 81; P. M. W. Robinson, "Stemmatic Analysis of the Fifteenth-century Witnesses to the Wife of Bath's Prologue," N. F. Blake and P. M. W. Robinson, eds., *The Canterbury Tales Project: Occasional Papers II* (Oxford: Office for Humanities Computing, 1997); E. Solopova, "The Problem of Authorial Variants in the Wife of Bath's Prologue," in the same volume.

original, supplied by one of his readers dissatisfied by the text of the first edition.[9] Unfortunately, Caxton did this correction very inconsistently, and this prevented scholars such as Manly and Rickert from seeing the second edition as a serious witness and making the most of its evidence. However, the information contained in the second edition, though scarce and fragmentary, turns out to be of exceptional value: it provides some of the missing links we badly need for understanding the relationship between the manuscripts. On the whole, as we learn more, the circle of important manuscripts tends to grow wider rather than narrower.

All the decisions we had to make in connection with our work were fraught with consequences. Once a project of this scale is started, it is difficult to go back. Had we overestimated our resources and set ourselves impossible tasks, the project would have failed. Decisions depend on one another and are always difficult to reverse. Reversal of decisions can mean lost weeks and months of effort, mistakes, and inconsistencies, painful transitions during which all involved in the project have to retrain their habits. The decision to transcribe all the manuscripts suggested many features of our transcription policy. We had to accept some limitations determined by our material, resources, and the time scale. Thus, initially, we wanted our transcripts to reflect the letter forms used by the scribes. Most Chaucer manuscripts employ spelling systems which allow several different forms of such letters as r, s, e, w and so on. However, distinguishing letter forms across the large range of texts that we had decided to transcribe proved impossible, because, apart from clearly recognized letter forms, the scribes used many intermediate forms difficult to attribute to a particular type. To try to impose a system on all this variety seemed too dangerous a plan, likely to involve us in unforeseen difficulties. Producing even a limited graphetic transcription also proved very time consuming and tended to increase the rate of error. To create electronic texts suitable for computer-assisted research we had to find a compromise between various sometimes contradictory requirements in order to achieve consistency and accuracy without sacrificing precision and richness.

To produce the first (and subsequent) CD-ROMs, to advance our research on the textual tradition, and to work our way right to the end of the project we have had to perform a number of laborious tasks. We have had to collect copies of all the manuscripts and pre-1500 printed editions. We have had to devise a system of transcription capable of coping with ambiguities of fifteenth-century spelling, with abbreviations and characters of uncertain

---

[9] B. Boyd, "William Caxton," in Ruggiers, *Editing Chaucer*, 13–34; N. F. Blake, "Caxton and Chaucer," in *Leeds Studies in English*, n.s., 1 (1967), 19–36.

semantic value, such as various flourishes and tails. We have had to transcribe every word of these manuscripts, using this system, into machine-readable form: some six million words in 30,000 pages in eighty-eight manuscripts. We have had to write software to compare all these versions, word by word, to see exactly how the manuscripts agree and disagree. Now, when some of this work has been completed, we can ask ourselves: is all the effort justified? Has it brought the expected results?

One justification of our work is the methods we have developed and the materials we have made available. The collation program Peter Robinson made for this work is now in use in many other text-editing projects.[10] Similarly, our experience of transcription has helped guide the formation of the primary text transcription encoding scheme outlined in the *Text Encoding Initiative Guidelines,* and this encoding has also been used by many other scholars.[11] The CD-ROM made available manuscript materials to researchers that were difficult or impossible to access before: now any reading in any manuscript or early printed edition of The Wife of Bath's Prologue can be easily accessed in transcript or in image. The materials published together on CD-ROM enrich our understanding of the fluctuating character of medieval textual traditions and facilitate the study of the development of language and of writing across the fifteenth century. One could also invoke the argument that the electronic critical edition is changing utterly the way in which we read, and to argue that the presentation of The Wife of Bath's Prologue on our first CD-ROM supposes a new way of reading. On it we present no less than 117 different versions of the text, all linked word by word with hypertext, with massive spelling databases and collations offering yet more ways into and through the text.

We are far from sure how people might read our electronic edition. One could even say that it is easier to edit a text in this manner than it will be for people to read and absorb all this. We have, however, given much thought and effort to the design of our CD-ROM in an attempt to make it user-friendly. We never considered it sufficient just to bring all the information together in the manner of the catalogue of dreams in *The House of Fame.*

---

[10] "*Collate:* A Program for Interactive Collation of Large Textual Traditions," in N. Ide and S. Hockey, *Research in Humanities Computing* 3 (Oxford: Oxford Univ. Press, 1994), 32–45.

[11] C. M. Sperberg–McQueen and L. Burnard, eds., *Guidelines for Electronic Text Encoding and Interchange* (Chicago and Oxford, 1994). Peter Robinson was responsible for the drafting of the chapter on transcription of primary textual materials in this volume, and many of the examples from the text are drawn from our work on The Wife of Bath's Prologue.

One's ability to absorb information depends on how the information is presented. We attempted to make sure that the structure of our edition is clear to the readers and that they can move easily and efficiently between its various parts. We tried to facilitate comparison of different aspects of the texts by linking transcripts, images and research tools together in various ways. We provided explanatory materials, such as descriptions of the manuscripts or transcription introductions, that tell exactly which features of the original the transcripts reflect and how, and which aspects they cannot reflect because of interpretation difficulties.[12] We provided special research tools such as regularized and unregularized collations and linguistic databases to assist textual and language research.

However, the most important question we can ask in order to evaluate the success of our work is: has it brought us closer to our aim of establishing Chaucer's text? Have the research methods that electronic editing made possible proved as promising as we hoped? To answer this question I will briefly summarize what we have learnt about the textual tradition of *The Canterbury Tales* and describe the methods we used to do this research.

The first sustained effort we made in the analysis of the textual tradition was a detailed metrical comparison I carried out of six important early manuscripts. This was much helped by having the texts in a machine-readable form. My experience of studying prosody suggests that metrical research is facilitated by a very simple resource: a lineated collation where lines from manuscripts are printed out in full one under the other. When one is comparing more than two manuscripts (for example, six, as I did), this becomes essential. Such presentation of texts can be difficult to achieve, but once the texts are available on a computer, Peter Robinson's *Collate* can produce this layout in minutes. The metrical values of the words in a line are interrelated: a substitution of one word changes the metrical status of words around it, and the prosodic structure of the whole line becomes different. Because of this, it is important to see the whole line when doing metrical research: trying to reconstruct the line mentally using variant readings as they are presented in critical apparatus of printed editions may lead to wrong conclusions.

Metrical analysis proved most valuable for the study of textual tradition. It turned out to be useful for identification of non-authorial intervention,

---

[12] See P. M. W. Robinson and E. Solopova, "Guidelines for Transcription of the Manuscripts of the Wife of Bath's Prologue," in N. F. Blake and P. M. W. Robinson, eds., *The Canterbury Tales Project: Occasional Papers I* (Oxford: Office for Humanities Communication, 1993), 19–52.

because the different editorial policies and scribal processes underlying the manuscripts reveal themselves in their attitudes to metrical form. Metrical analysis of the earliest manuscripts contributed to the debate about the textual value of the two most important manuscripts of the *Tales*: it demonstrated that, contrary to what was earlier widely accepted, the Hengwrt manuscript is metrically more regular than Ellesmere for The Wife of Bath's Prologue.[13] It has also shown that Ellesmere in The Wife of Bath's Prologue lacks metrical regularity because it shares parts of its text with a group of manuscripts that go back to a source that at some early stage underwent an obviously non-authorial stylistic revision. This revision was an attempt to make the style more formal, more prosaic, and less conversational, to regularize grammar and to clean up what were perceived as inconsistencies in Chaucer's text. Concerned with style, the reviser was completely indifferent to prosody: correcting the style he often damaged the meter. Metrical comparison helped to investigate relations within the group of manuscripts that share this stylistic revision, and to clarify the attitudes of individual scribes to the style and meter of their texts. Apart from Ellesmere in parts of its text, two other influential early manuscripts, Cambridge University Library Gg.4.27 and London, British Library, MS Harley 7334, are based on this revised exemplar.

I did this work in 1994, before we had finished the transcription and collation of all the manuscripts. Once we had achieved these, it was possible for Peter Robinson to use the methods of cladistic and database analysis that he had developed for this work on all the information about manuscript agreements and disagreements. Cladistic analysis is performed by software originally developed by evolutionary biologists.[14] Working from the patterns of agreements and disagreements which emerge from the collation of the manuscripts, cladistic analysis builds a stemma which shows how the manuscripts are related. Database analysis allows us to see exactly which readings in which lines are shared by any combination of manuscripts (Robinson, "Stemmatic Analysis"). It proved indispensable for making judgments about common ancestors of groups of manuscripts, and for reconstructing the readings contained in these remote and now lost exemplars. As well as confirming the existence

---

[13] E. Solopova, "Chaucer's Metre and Scribal Editing in the Early Manuscripts of the *Canterbury Tales*," in Blake and Robinson, eds., *The Canterbury Tales Project: Occasional Papers II* (Oxford: Office for Humanities Computing, 1997).

[14] P. M. W. Robinson and R. J. O'Hara, "Computer-Assisted Methods of Stemmatic Analysis," in Blake and Robinson, eds., *The Canterbury Tales Project: Occasional Papers I*, 53–74.

of the four manuscript groupings discovered by Manly and Rickert, groups A, B, C, and D, Robinson clarified the status of two other groups posited by Manly and Rickert. He demonstrated that these groups, which he named E and F, are independent of the other manuscript groupings but appear to descend from a common source. Group E is the group, based on a stylistically revised exemplar, that I studied as a part of my research on meter. It follows from this analysis that Ellesmere and other manuscripts of group E are removed by at least two stages of scribal copying from Chaucer's original. All this again shifts the evidence in favor of Hengwrt as a better witness of Chaucer's text, and it means that the tens of thousands of students who every year read *The Canterbury Tales* in the *Riverside Chaucer,* based on Ellesmere, are reading a text at many points far removed from what Chaucer is likely to have written.

When we started computer-assisted research on the textual tradition, we were concerned that the value of cladistic analysis would be limited, because it would not be able to cope with manuscript contamination. However, Peter Robinson demonstrated that cladistic analysis can be actually used to determine and confirm contamination ("Stemmatic Analysis"). Producing cladograms for every one hundred lines of The Wife of Bath's Prologue, he showed that some manuscripts change affiliations and appear in different places in the stemma for different sections of the text. The only explanation for this is that the scribe used several exemplars to produce a given text. Fifteen manuscripts were identified as extensively contaminated and excluded from the genealogical stemma—a step of exceptional importance in the investigation of the textual tradition.

Another study assisted by cladistic analysis is my research on punctuation in the manuscripts of The Wife of Bath's Prologue.[15] It was generally accepted by scholars that punctuation in Chaucer manuscripts is not authorial and was entirely introduced by the scribes. This view relied on a study concerned primarily with punctuation in just two Chaucer manuscripts—Hengwrt and Ellesmere. When I started comparing punctuation in these two witnesses to that in all other manuscripts of The Wife of Bath's Prologue, I noticed that other manuscripts regularly agree between themselves and against Hengwrt and Ellesmere. This was further confirmed when cladistic analysis of all the variants, including punctuation variants, in all the extant witnesses of the

---

[15] "The Survival of Chaucer's Punctuation in the Early Manuscripts of the *Canterbury Tales,*" forthcoming in the Proceedings of the 1996 York Medieval Texts Conference, ed. A. J. Minnis.

Prologue, showed that five textually unrelated manuscripts formed a tight group distinguished from all the rest of the manuscripts, purely on the basis of their agreements in punctuation variants. This similarity of punctuation, which can not be explained by common exemplars, pointed to some important tendencies of scribal punctuation. Further research demonstrated that punctuation practice in Hengwrt and Ellesmere is unique among the fifteenth-century witnesses. The skill in the interpretation of the text and the rhetorical orientation of this punctuation strongly suggest its authorial origin. Certain features of this punctuation practice completely escaped scribal imitation: none of the fifteenth-century scribes was able to reproduce it exactly as it is found in Hengwrt and Ellesmere. The scribes' imitation of the original punctuation tended towards the mechanical, debasing its highly meaningful approach to the text. The likelihood that Chaucer's punctuation has survived in Hengwrt and Ellesmere has important implications for future editors of *The Canterbury Tales:* modern punctuation in the editions should take into account, whenever possible, the punctuation in these two best witnesses.

One of the most difficult problems which we had to confront is the possibility of authorial revision in Chaucer's text. As is well known, though the texts of Hengwrt and Ellesmere are very close in the second part of The Wife of Bath's Prologue, Hengwrt does not contain five passages present in many other manuscripts, including Ellesmere. Scholars have earlier suggested that these five passages were authorial and were present in Chaucer's working copy but were possibly written somewhere in the margins or marked for deletion.[16] Peter Robinson supposed that, since taken together, these thirty-two lines coarsen the portrayal of the Wife of Bath and show her as promiscuous and vulgar, as does no other part of the Prologue, these lines were composed when Chaucer intended to allocate what is now the Shipman's Tale to the Wife of Bath ("Stemmatic Analysis"). However, when Chaucer decided to give the Wife the much more genteel and subtle tale she now has, he saw that these lines were inappropriate and deleted them.

Our major difficulty was explaining the distribution of the passages: they seemed to be randomly scattered across the tradition and to occur in the manuscripts which were previously believed to be unrelated. Our research pointed to a simpler picture of the distribution of the passages: all the manu-

---

[16] J. S. P. Tatlock, "The *Canterbury Tales* in 1400," *PMLA* 50 (1935), 102; N. F. Blake, *The Textual Tradition of the Canterbury Tales* (London: Arnold, 1985), 44–57; N. F. Blake, "Geoffrey Chaucer: Textual Transmission and Editing," in A. J. Minnis and C. Brewer, *Crux and Controversy in Middle English Textual Criticism* (Cambridge: D. S. Brewer, 1992), 32.

scripts where the presence of the passages can not be explained by contamination appear to go back to a common exemplar. This conclusion rests on the
study of the texts of the passages themselves, as well as on the study of the
relationship between the manuscripts in which they are contained. My
research on the text of the passages indicates that the only manuscripts that
have the passages through direct ancestral descent and not through contamination are the AB group manuscripts, Ellesmere, Cambridge University Library Dd.4.24, and the manuscript used by Caxton for his second edition of
the *Tales* ("The Problem of Authorial Variants"). Peter Robinson's analysis
suggests that all these manuscripts, including the now lost source of Caxton's
corrections in his second edition, go back to one exemplar ("Stemmatic
Analysis"). Thus, we believe that there were at least two separate copies of
the text of The Wife of Bath's Prologue near the beginning of the whole
tradition: the exemplar of Hengwrt and manuscripts close to it, which had no
added passages, and what we call the alpha exemplar—the common ancestor
of Ellesmere, Cambridge University Library Dd.4.24, the AB manuscripts, and
the manuscript used by Caxton for his second edition. We do not know yet
what was the exact nature of the two archetypes. It seems likely, however,
that their texts were very close, just as Hengwrt and Ellesmere are close in the
second part of The Wife of Bath's Prologue. The presence or the absence of
the passages could have been the main or even the only distinction between
the two archetypes.

Our search for other examples of authorial revision in The Wife of Bath's
Prologue, apart from the "added passages," yielded little evidence. One reading that could be interpreted as a result of revision due to Chaucer's gradual
assimilation of his sources, is the first line of the Prologue, where some manuscripts have the word "experience," others "experiment." The Prologue opens
with:

> Experience, though noon auctoritee
> Were in this world, is right ynogh for me
> To speke of wo that is in mariage.

The use of "experiment" in this passage might appear to be a scribal mistake.
However, the source for this passage closely translated by Chaucer—a passage
from Jean de Meun's *Roman de la Rose*—also uses the word "experiment":

> Bele ere, juenne, nice et fole,
> N'ainc ne fui d'amour a escole,
> (Ou l'on seust la theorique;
> Mais je sai tout par la pratique:)
> **Experimenz** m'en ont fait sage,

> Que j'ai hantez tout mon aage.
> (12805–12810)[17]

It is possible that Chaucer's copy contained, interlineated or in the margins, variants he first used in his translation of the French text and then rejected as he moved further away from his source. Some of these authorial variants could have found their way into the surviving manuscripts. The possibility that "experiment" is an authorial variant does not mean, however, that Chaucer's meaning at any stage was "experiment" in the modern sense. In both English and French of this period the meaning and usage of "experiment" and "experience" appears to have been the same.[18]

The implications of our work are far-reaching. It suggests that while the text of Hengwrt is the best witness for the *Tales,* there is material, such as the added passages, which we believe to be authorial and which Hengwrt does not include. While Hengwrt may still be the best source for a scholarly edition, it is not the unique source and should be used with caution. We do not know yet its precise relation to Chaucer's original nor how likely it is to contain error. But we are aware, for example, that the Hengwrt and Ellesmere scribe was fairly indifferent to meter and could damage it: unique variants in both manuscripts sometimes represent the loss of metrically important words. We think that at several points in The Wife of Bath's Prologue readings from other manuscripts better reflect what Chaucer wrote than does Hengwrt. It is also possible that the producers of the Hengwrt manuscript have omitted or edited, for whatever reason, material that Chaucer wrote and intended for inclusion in the *Tales.*

Our study suggests that future editors should look beyond Hengwrt. Particularly promising is a group of some ten manuscripts which Peter Robinson's cladistic analysis showed to be close to Hengwrt and thus to Chaucer's original ("Stemmatic Analysis"). We believe that it is possible, through comparative

---

[17] A. Strubel, ed., *Guillaume de Lorris et Jean de Meun Le Roman de la Rose* (Paris: Le Livre de Poche, 1992).

[18] See *Oxford English Dictionary,* entries for "experiment" and "experience," and the entries for "experientia" and "experimentum" in R. E. Latham and D. R. Howlett, comps., *Dictionary of Medieval Latin from British Sources* (London: Oxford Univ. Press, 1975–1986; in progress). Chaucer's usual word and the only word registered in J. S. P. Tatlock and A. G. Kennedy, *A Concordance to the Complete Works of Geoffrey Chaucer and to the Romaunt of the Rose* (Washington, DC: The Carnegie Institution of Washington, 1927), and in N. F. Blake et al., *A New Concordance to The Canterbury Tales based on Blake's text edited from the Hengwrt manuscript* (Okayama: Univ. Education Press, 1994) is "experience."

study of these, to reconstruct the state of Chaucer's working copy as he left it, and as it came to its first copyists.

Investigation of the relations between the manuscripts and of various processes within the textual tradition, including contamination, the possibility of revision, and changes to meter and punctuation, requires that we have quick access to large bodies of material. We have to use collations to evaluate the manuscript support for any particular reading, the results of cladistic analysis to see how the manuscripts that contain this reading are related, and the database analysis to see what other readings are shared by these witnesses. We have to look at manuscripts that in the past hardly ever attracted the interest of scholars. We are glad that our initial vision of the scope and uses of an electronic edition was broad enough to provide for all these various types of research, including many we initially did not anticipate. I return to the title of this paper: is all this effort of editing all the manuscripts of *The Canterbury Tales* in electronic form worthwhile? In the last year, we have learnt far more about the textual tradition of the whole *Canterbury Tales,* through the one small window of The Wife of Bath's Prologue, than we had dared to hope.

The Application of Digital Image Processing to the Analysis of Watermarked Paper and Printers' Ornament Usage in Early Printed Books

DAVID L. GANTS

I. Introduction

FIFTY YEARS AND TWO DAYS AGO, CHARLTON HINMAN REPORTED the results of some work he had been pursuing before a section of the Modern Language Association's annual meeting.[1] As conference papers go it was rather modest: it did not present any new insights into or interpretations of a literary work or genre. Instead, it demonstrated the possibility of applying optical and mechanical technologies used by Hinman and others in Naval Intelligence during World War II to the textual collation of sixteenth- and seventeenth-century printed books. In a rather anecdotal fashion, Hinman talked about building his prototype collator out of "ordinary microfilm projectors (borrowed from the Navy), some pieces of a wooden apple box (abstracted from a trash pile), some heavy cardboard (begged from the Folger bindery), and parts of a rusty Erector set (more or less hi-jacked from the small son of a close personal friend)."[2]

---

[1] For further details on the papers presented see *PMLA* 46 (1946): 1353.

[2] Charlton Hinman, "Mechanized Collation: A Preliminary Report," *PBSA* 41 (1947): 102.

Many of you here today are familiar with the results of Hinman's work in textual analysis. He went on to develop a series of machines that came to bear his name, one version of which is still in use at the Folger Shakespeare Library. With these instruments he and other scholars reinvigorated the textual study of early modern literature. The traditional scholarly edition as described in current MLA guidelines could not exist without the rapid, accurate, mechanical collation of multiple copies made possible by Hinman.

Recently, scholars working in the field of bibliographical studies have begun experimenting with a number of digital tools that, like Hinman's collator, have the potential to alter the manner in which we investigate and understand the past. The introduction of powerful, affordable microcomputer technology into our discipline has made possible the reproduction, enhancement, and analysis of physical evidence at a scale unimaginable just ten years ago. Today I'd like to discuss one facet of this continuing research: the application of digital image processing to the study of watermarked paper and typographic material in early printed books. Using equipment available in most retail electronics shops or through computer catalogues, I'll demonstrate some of the ways that scholars are developing fresh approaches to old problems and, I hope, spark new ideas among some of you in the audience.

II. Watermarks

European papermakers first started using watermarks as far back as the twelfth or thirteenth centuries. These artisans discovered that by placing a wire profile on the face of a paper mould they could create various figures in the sheet, images which emerged when lit from behind. As objects of study, however, watermarks have proven tantalizingly elusive. Approximately 100 years ago, scholars such as W. A. Briquet and C. M. Churchill began cataloguing and classifying watermarked paper, reproducing the images they found by sketching free-hand or tracing onto a separate sheet the unicorns and pots and fleur-de-lis they encountered (illustration 1).

Their collections of marks represent countless hours of painstaking work, but the lack of accuracy inherent in the sketching process has limited their usefulness to bibliographical researchers. In the 1950s, Soviet scientists perfected a process that produced clear, accurate contact prints of watermarks using a radioactive beta source and X-ray film, the so-called beta radiography method (illustration 2).

This procedure delivers wonderful images, but the expense of the materials and restrictions placed on them by governmental agencies have limited its widespread use. Recent years have witnessed a number of alternative techniques for the study of watermarks, including the Ilkley Method of contact

Illustration 1: Sketch #576 from Edward Heywood,
Watermarks, Mainly of the 17th and 18th Centuries (Hilversum, 1950).

Illustration 2: Beta radiograph taken from leaf B4 of
The Workes of Beniamin Jonson (London, 1616),
Huntington Library, San Marino, CA, call number 62101.

photo-reproduction, and Thomas Gravell's use of Dylux, a proofing medium from the print industry. These new methods have expanded the researcher's ability to reproduce and hence study paper usage in the early printing trade by introducing techniques one can perform on location in a rare book reading room or archive.

Emerging digital technology has advanced our ability to investigate paper evidence to a new level, building upon the work of Gravell and others. Using flatbed and hand-held digital scanners we can take images created by earlier technologies such as beta radiography or Dylux, convert them into digital form, and, with the aid of a computer, apply various image-manipulation routines. Notice how much clearer the Dylux reproduction appears after a series of enhancements done with an off-the-shelf software package (illustration 3).

Even more exciting has been the rapid drop in the price of digital cameras over the past year. While existing methods of capturing watermark images produce monochromatic reproductions, digital cameras generate high resolution, full color images and thus provide many greater possibilities for computer manipulation. Some institutions have opened their own digital centers equipped with stationary cameras capable of generating images of 5000 x 7000 pixels and with 24-bit color depth. This watermark image from the 1640 collected works of Ben Jonson was taken at the University of Virginia's special collections library, using a Kontron digital camera (illustration 4).

Because of the extraordinary resolution and depth of color map it is possible to enhance this image at the pixel-by-pixel level, making the obscuring types blend into the background and bringing out clearly the desired watermark.[3]

Such resources are not limited to large institutions, however: small, portable and inexpensive cameras attach directly to a laptop, and when combined with a flexible light source can be used by an individual scholar in a reading room to collect images quickly and safely. This image, taken from the 1616 Jonson Folio with a portable camera, shows the possibilities afforded by such technology (illustration 5).

While portable cameras at present have a relatively small resolution capacity, limited to 640 x 480 pixels, they do capture images very quickly. The resulting images are small (less than 50 kilobytes), and as they take very little

---

[3] Fotoscientifica S.N.C. of Parma, Italy, has developed a similar system employing a digital camera with a maximum image resolution of 6000 x 7520 pixels and enhancement software capable of extremely fine color-map manipulations.

Illustration 3: Dylux reproduction taken from leaf F1 of
The Workes of Beniamin Jonson (London, 1616), Folger Shakespeare Library,
Washington, DC, call number STC 14751.2, copy 1.

Illustration 4: Black-and-white print of original
24-bit color digital image, Kontron camera. Leaf 3L1,
The Workes of Beniamin Jonson (London, 1640), author's personal copy.

Illustration 5: Black-and-white print of original
24-bit color digital image, Connectix Color QuickCam. Leaf G6,
The Workes of Beniamin Jonson (London, 1616), author's personal copy.

time to produce, a scholar can in an afternoon collect an amount of evidence
that would have taken Briquet weeks to sketch.[4]

III. Typography

The study of watermarks and paper is not the only area to have seen exciting
changes due to the application of new technologies. For some time scholars
have examined the ornaments, borders, and individual types used in printing
houses to recognize patterns of composition, imposition and machining, and
to identify the particular printer or printers responsible for a work. Those of
you who have worked with Hinman's collating machine will recall the three
optical scopes protruding down from the eyepiece, each providing a different

---

[4] At this point a digital image of the audience was taken using a Connectix Color
QuickCam attached to a Pentium laptop employing proprietary QuickPict software.

level of magnification. Hinman employed these scopes to identify the recurrent use of typographic material in the Jaggard shop. He discovered, among other things, that the Shakespeare Folio was set by formes, an insight which had important consequences for modern editors.

As with watermarks, the study of typographic material has always been hindered by the problem of gathering and organizing evidence. Hinman sketched each distinctly damaged type he encountered on an index card, producing a large catalogue of types to which he referred as he progressed in his investigations. Such a painstaking and time-consuming process severely limits the progress of a study, whether large or small. Additionally, because what appears on the page is not the type itself but only the ink left behind when the metal form bit into the paper, the image we see has been subjected to a number of distorting factors, the most troublesome of which is called ink squeeze. When the face of the type is pressed down into the paper, the layer of ink the type bears flattens and spreads outward in all directions as it transfers to the sheet, obscuring the original metal image. Only under high magnification can we distinguish the face of the type from the ink squeeze surrounding it.

The application of digital technology delivers innovative solutions to these problems by giving us new ways of looking at the evidence. High-resolution color scans of early printed materials produce images rich in detail that stand up to extreme magnification and modification. Here are three instances of what may or may not be a single drop capital used by William Stansby in the latter half of the 1610s. When placed side-by-side, two areas in particular seem to show progressive damage: the dent on the top of the character and the wearing down of the deformation at the bottom (illustration 6).

If we zoom in on just the latter area, some differences and similarities begin to emerge: note that the dimensions and alignment of first line up well, for example, but neither correlates with the third (illustration 7).

While magnification allows us to compare small sections of the types, we can also make a simple movie to illustrate how the types compare in their overall shape.[5] Here the shift in overall size and relative thickness of lower right section of the counter again link the first two images but not the third. These brief tests seem to indicate that the first two samples have strong correlations, justifying more detailed analysis, while the third sample can be ruled out. I've only used three images, but one could easily expand the sample

---

[5] At this point the speaker showed a digital movie consisting of three images flashing on the screen in rapid succession.

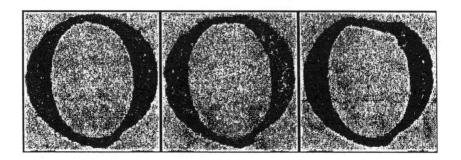

Illustration 6: The sample drop capitals were taken from
A Merrie Dialogue Betweene Band, Cuffe, and Ruffe (1615), *The Workes
of Beniamin Jonson* (1616), and Samuel Purchas, *Purchas his Pilgrimage* (1617).

Illustration 7: Detail of lower-left sections of drop capitals.

population to a dozen or more, as the testing process moves ahead swiftly once the evidence has been collected.

IV. Ornaments

In order to generate such a sequence of images, I employed a Hewlett Packard flatbed scanner, a tabletop mechanism that works along the lines of a photocopy machine. However, a number of hand-held scanners are now on the market, devices which, as with the portable digital camera, attach directly to laptop computers for use in the field. Having a portable scanner available greatly expands the type and quality of evidence one can gather, and allows one to exploit serendipitous occurrences. For example, while working at the Folger Shakespeare Library I came across an autograph dedication by Ben Jonson in a volume of William Camden's works and was able to scan it for reference purposes (illustration 8).

The images these devices create are of a much higher resolution than those coming from small digital cameras, which makes them quite useful when studying printers' ornaments and other decorative materials found in books from the incunabula period through today. Here, for example, are three instances of a small ornamental letter used by William Stansby in the middle part of the 1610s (illustration 9).

By placing them side-by-side one can begin to see progressive damage manifest itself on the raised wooden edges that make up the ornament. Notice the progressive damage on the crossbar as well as the lower left serif. As with the metal types we can also isolate details for closer study or make movies illustrating the fashion in which this piece deteriorates.

Additionally, digital scans can help distinguish between quite similar ornaments of the same design by identifying those areas where variations might occur. These headpieces appear in two large folio volumes published in 1616, the collected works of King James (printed by Robert Barker and John Bill), and of Ben Jonson (printed by William Stansby; illustration 10).

This is a very popular design and is found in a number of works from this period, including the First Folio of Shakespeare. When examining two books from different printing houses, both of which employ what appears to be the same ornamental headpiece, we need to examine those pieces very carefully. If they are indeed the same, then their use by different establishments may signal a case of shared printing. If they are different, then we know that these houses had two copies taken from the same design and can look out for them in the future. With such an intricate piece a scholar might spend a great deal of time going back and forth in tennis fashion, looking for similarities or differences. When the scans are viewed as a simple two-frame movie the points

Illustration 8: Scanned Jonson autograph.

Illustration 9: Ornamental characters scanned from Edward Topsell's
Times Lamentation (1613), *The Workes of Beniamin Jonson* (1616), and
The French Kings Declaration Against the Dukes of Vendosme and Mayenne (1617).

Illustration 10: Ornamental headpieces appearing in (top) *The Workes of the Most High and Mighty Prince, James* (London, 1616), and (bottom) *The Workes of Beniamin Jonson* (London, 1616).

of interest quickly become apparent.[6] In particular, note the change in the right stag's leg and the shifting cross–hatches on the left archer's body. This simple test demonstrates that indeed these are two distinct ornaments created from the same design.

V. Control

While technologies such as those I've demonstrated enhance tremendously our ability to collect data, they also challenge us to take control of the vast amount of information at our disposal. A project can amass megabytes of images and yet flounder because the evidence is not collected and organized in a fashion that allows full investigation. Furthermore, if those megabytes are in a proprietary format, those outside the project who might wish to share the information but use a different computing platform are effectively shut out.

Fortunately, a great deal of work has already been done to address these concerns, much of it centering on a set of encoding guidelines with which you may be familiar: Standard Generalized Markup Language. SGML has three particular strengths that lend themselves to the control and exchange of bibliographical and textual data. First, it is descriptive, employing simple codes to categorize structural elements of a document. Second, it is referential, allowing the scholar to establish pointers or links to related elements within a single document or among a group of documents. Third, it is analytical in that it provides a means to encode higher-level annotational information into the data.

Beyond SGML's descriptive, referential, and analytical strengths, the system offers platform independence as well. It employs no binary information, just the characters found on a simple keyboard, and it contains a mechanism for string substitution, that is, "a simple machine-independent way of stating that a particular string of characters in the document should be replaced by some other string when the document is processed."[7] This means, among other things, that SGML can represent a broad range of character sets such as Cyrillic or Greek.

The flexibility and power SGML brings to bibliographical studies are immense. For example, look at this title page from the Jonson Folio of 1616 (illustration 11).

---

[6] At this point, the speaker showed a digital movie consisting of two images flashing on the screen in rapid succession.

[7] *Guidelines for Electronic Text Encoding and Interchange*, eds. C. M. Sperberg–McQueen and Lou Burnard (Chicago, 1994), 15.

Euery

MAN IN

HIS

HVMOVR.

A Comœdie.

Acted in the yeere 1598. By the then
Lord Chamberlaine his
Seruants.

The Author B. I.

IUVEN.

Haud tamen inuideas vati, quem pulpita pascunt.

LONDON,

Printed by WILLIAM STANSBY.

M. DC. XVI.

Illustration 11: Sig. A1ʳ, *The Workes of Beniamin Jonson* (London, 1616).

There are a number of classes of information that we can extract from this page for analysis: paper and watermarks, typographical material, textual variants. In addition, descriptive bibliographers express the text of a title page in prose through a process called quasi-facsimile title-page transcription. SGML provides a way to combine all these disparate classes of evidence into database form that can then be combined with other related evidence to create a single, cross-referential resource.

The process might begin with the conversion of the title-page text into straight ASCII characters:

Euery MAN IN HIS HVMOVR. A Comoedie. Acted in the yeere 1598. By the then Lord Chamberlaine his Seruants. The Author B.I. IUVEN. Haud tamen inuideas vati, quem pulpita pascunt. LONDON, Printed by WILLIAM STANSBY. M. D C. XVI.

To these are added basic structural and format tagging, such things as line definitions and typeface:

<div type="title-page" n=2a>Euery <lb> MAN IN <lb> HIS <lb> HVMOVR.<lb> <hi rend="italic">A Comoedie</hi>. <lb> Acted in the yeere 1598. By the then <lb> Lord Chamberlaine his <lb> Seruants. <lb>The Author B.I. <lb> IUVEN. <lb> <hi rend= "italic">Haud tamen inuideas vati, quem pulpita pascunt</hi>. <lb> <figure type="rule" rend="single" n=75> L<hi rend="small cap">ONDON</hi>, <lb> Printed by W<hi rend="small cap">ILLIAM</hi> S<hi rend="small cap">TANSBY</hi>. <lb> <figure type="rule" rend="single" n=37> M. D C. XVI. </div>

Next we insert between the initial <div> and the text an element that establishes a cross-reference to the section of the database containing information on the paper:

<div type="title-page" n=2a>
    <head>
        <note type="paper"><xref n="wm002"> Regular
            paper, class 02 </xref>
        </note>
    </head> etc.

Following this comes numerous references to textual variants, alternate title pages used in the folio, specific fonts of type used on each line, all of which becomes much too complex to show today. Out of this long sequence, from the examination of primary documents to the encoding of annotational information, comes a sophisticated digital database that can be used on almost any platform with a variety of search and display packages. Furthermore, since HTML (HyperText Mark-up Language), the encoding scheme currently in use on the World Wide Web, is itself a small installation of the larger SGML framework, the database can be mounted on a Web server and the results displayed in real time across the Internet, using an SGML-to-HTML conversion filter. A number of projects employing schemes similar to the one I just described are now well under way, notably Daniel Mosser and Ernest Sullivan's Thomas L. Gravell Watermark Archive at Virginia Tech, and Robert Allison's Archive of Papers and Watermarks in Greek Manuscripts at Bates College. In the next few years we should see an explosion of very exciting work.

VI. Conclusion

In the fifty years since Hinman's initial MLA report, the theory and practice of textual collation has changed in significant ways; more sophisticated and portable machines have superseded the first contraption made of packing materials and a child's toy. So too will devices and techniques not yet imagined replace our scanners and cameras and copies of Adobe Photoshop. The computer industry, fueled by a fervent belief in the myth of progress as embodied in Moore's Law, will continue devising ever-more powerful machines. This will in turn enable bibliographers and critics to gather greater amounts of physical evidence, organize that evidence with greater efficiency, and analyze the resulting data with ever-greater imagination and ingenuity, to the end that we will gain a clearer understanding of those texts handed down to us from the culture that flourished during the English Renaissance.

Electronic Editions and the
Needs of Readers

JOHN LAVAGNINO

A LTHOUGH VERY FEW ELECTRONIC EDITIONS WITH ANY SCHOL-
arly pretensions exist today, there is already a dominant idea of
what an electronic edition ought to be. The idea is that an electronic
edition ought to be an archive. It should offer diplomatic transcriptions of
documents, and facsimiles of those documents. And it should avoid many of
the things that scholarly editions have traditionally done, particularly the creation of critically edited texts by means of editorial emendation. On this view,
what readers need is access to original sources—to as many of them as possible, avoiding as much as possible the shaping and selection that editors have
traditionally engaged in. Although a lot of archives in the world were created
and shaped to make specific points, this kind of archive-edition is not con-
ceived of as doing that: it is instead imagined as a neutral witness.[1] (And let

---

[1] In English-language editing, this doctrine is strongest among those working with
texts published after the Renaissance; for some examples, see: A. Walton Litz, "After-
word," in Richard J. Finneran, editor, *The Literary Text in the Digital Age* (Ann Arbor:
Univ. of Michigan Press, 1996), 245–248; Jerome McGann, "The Complete Writings
and Pictures of Dante Gabriel Rossetti: A Hypermedia Research Archive," TEXT 7
(1994): 95–105; G. Thomas Tanselle, "Critical Editions, Hypertexts, and Genetic Criticism," *Romanic Review* 86:3 (May 1995): 581–593; and David Womersley, "Delight-
ful Ways to Cheat Learning," *Times Higher Education Supplement* (14 June 1996): vii.
Within Renaissance studies, this point of view is less widespread to date, in part because there is comparatively little work being conducted to create electronic editions

me point out that, as the talk by Elizabeth Solopova makes clear, the *Canterbury Tales* Project *does* intend to work towards establishing a new text of Chaucer; it's a lot more than merely creating an archive.)

The archive model has its merits, and indeed its methodology is in part derived from the tradition of scholarly editing: there are obvious connections to the approach of the Malone Society's reprint series, for example. Access to original sources is certainly a good thing. But I don't think it's the only good thing an edition can do, and some of the other good things are especially important when we're working with Renaissance texts. Readers need more than just an archive when working with Renaissance texts, because the archive can give us only a limited representation of these texts.

Since Peter Robinson's not here, I can steal his trick[2] of talking about the subject at hand by describing two different editions I'm working on: in my case, these will be the Thomas Middleton edition and the corpus of Renaissance texts from the Women Writers Project.

The Middleton edition is an edition of Middleton's plays, poems, and pamphlets, in modern spelling, for the most part, and with full textual and explanatory notes. It's going to be published by Oxford in both print and electronic forms; Gary Taylor is the general editor, but there are something like six dozen of us working on various aspects of it. The principal aim of the edition is to change the way we see Middleton by making readily available the results not only of our own research but also that of the last few decades of scholarship.

One comment I've often heard over the past few years, especially because I'm handling the computer side of the operation, has been that we ought to include the archive too: that we ought to be doing a documentary edition alongside the critical edition. As it stands, our edition will offer only critically

---

of texts of this period; but see Michael Warren, "The Theatricalization of Text: Beckett, Jonson, Shakespeare," *Library Chronicle of the University of Texas at Austin* 20:1/2 (1990): 39–59. And Michael Leslie, "Electronic Editions and the Hierarchy of Texts," in *The Politics of the Electronic Text*, ed. Warren Chernaik, Caroline Davis, and Marilyn Deegan (Oxford: Office for Humanities Computing, 1993), 41–51, specifically rules out offering any sort of indexing to a large and varied collection of seventeenth-century letters in electronic transcription, on the grounds that an index imposes an interpretation. More generally, the "anti-editing" movement implies this sort of electronic edition, even when electronic editions are not the specific subject; see Warren's writings, and those of Randall McLeod, such as "Information upon Information," *TEXT* 5 (1991): 241–281.

[2] See, for example, "Two Contrasting Electronic Editions: *The Collected Voltaire* and the *Canterbury Tales*," paper presented at the Modern Language Association Convention, San Diego, California, 29 December 1994.

edited texts. And that's true of the electronic version too, whose contents will be identical to those of the print version. For readers, the principal advantages of the electronic version will be the ease of searching the text (and the introductions and annotations), and the ease of following cross-references from one text to another.

Our edition does not include the archive because it seems less important to us than what we *are* doing, and because the preparation of the archive takes time and money that we prefer to devote to other ends. It would be nice to have, but we don't think it would be especially effective in changing Middleton's stature in the world.

Another reason is that the archive is actually available already. For example, there is a microfilm archive of Middleton's works that you can buy from University Microfilms and that many universities have. It's true that they throw in tens of thousands of other books, but almost all of the early printed texts by Middleton are in it. Of the 119 STC and Wing items with writing in them by Middleton, only sixteen are not currently available as part of the STC, Wing, or Thomason microfilm collections, and most of these are quite minor variants of items that are included. (Six of them are variants of the second and third Shakespeare folios, for example.) Such an archive necessarily excludes materials that survive only in manuscript—such as *The Second Maiden's Tragedy* and *The Witch*—but if access to the original sources is what you want, then this does do the job pretty well. And since it's relevant to our theme today, let me point out that sixty years ago microfilm was the exciting new information technology. David Gants has alluded to the role it played in Charlton Hinman's work, and generally people said about it many of the same things you now hear said about computers, the Internet, and the World Wide Web.[3]

But the archive is available in electronic form, too. Chadwyck–Healey can provide collections of electronic texts, based on the field as defined in the *New Cambridge Bibliography of English Literature*, that include thirty-nine of the fifty-nine works that our edition will include. Many of the missing works are prose pamphlets, a kind of writing they don't claim to cover yet; if you look only at dramatic works, they've got thirty-five out of forty-one.

These archives are useful—I've certainly found them so in my work on our edition. But they're also limited. They're limited because they don't go beyond *utility* to the attempt to change our *understanding* of these texts. Or, to be more precise: these archives, like the bibliographies and catalogues on

---

[3] See James M. Nyce and Paul Kahn, eds., *From Memex to Hypertext: Vannevar Bush and the Mind's Machine* (Boston: Academic Press, 1991).

which they're based, are directed towards changing our understanding of the whole range of printed texts over a long period. That's a good thing, and they do it well, but it's only one aspect of what's involved in changing our perception of individual authors or works.

One aim of our edition is the creation of a better image of Middleton as a writer. Creating such an image is not something that the STC or Wing do especially well for any writer, because of their orientation towards cataloguing printed output: if we know a work was written or performed decades before its publication, these catalogues typically will not inform you, because it's not their job; they simply give publication dates. And though they try to indicate attributions of works other than those asserted by the books themselves, this also is not a function they can possibly do as thoroughly as those who set their minds to working on the canon of a particular author. Consequently, to generate my figures about Middleton works on the STC and Wing microfilms, I had to collect information from a good many headings, and not just the "Middleton" heading. It's a picture *I* created, not one that this archive is already offering me.

Chadwyck–Healey used the *New Cambridge Bibliography of English Literature* as their guide in creating their databases. This means that their "Middleton" heading does actually collect most of their Middleton items. They attribute *The Revenger's Tragedy* to Middleton, which is still rather unusual even for print editions (though their actual text of the work seems to be making the suggestion that Tourneur's name appears somewhere on the original publication, which isn't the case). The dates you see for works in the Chadwyck–Healey database are also sometimes odd, because they're the dates of the printed editions they used. Hence *The Second Maiden's Tragedy* gets a date of 1909, and *The Witch* gets 1945. (In cases like these, they do seem to have provided dates of composition in notes to the text itself, but it's these odd publication dates that you see in any listing of the database's contents.)

But they could always change these names and dates without great effort. There's a bigger problem, which is that a simple list of works and dates is not enough to represent any considered judgment about authorship and dating of works in this period. Because of the difficulty of such determinations, it's essential to have an exposition that gives the evidence and reasoning involved, and makes clear the degree of certainty of the conclusions—which, of course, is why such an exposition is a standard feature in editions of Renaissance plays.

So creating an image of the author requires more than a mere listing of works and dates. And, for that matter, if your aim is to modify ideas of authorship, the same move from an archive to a presentation that involves the overt presence of a scholar's mediation is necessary, because the message of a list of authors and titles is that these authors sat alone in their rooms and created these works from pure imagination. That is the common popular view of authorship today, and without specific arguments against it there's no real pressure on anyone who holds it to think differently.

Another aim of our edition is to foster the understanding of Middleton's writings. In this respect as well, the simple archive doesn't work very well, because it has no way to transmit most kinds of scholarly understanding of texts as literary works. And readers are known to need and want this information. The popularity of the Arden Shakespeare series, for example, derives far more from its annotation than from the text or textual notes. (That's not just my impression—back when Routledge was planning the third series of the Arden Shakespeare, they did market research to find out what their customers wanted. Textual apparatus came dead last in the scale of importance of various features, which is why it's migrated to the base of the page in the new series.[4])

It's at least possible to add to an archive annotation, introductions, and discussions of the relationships between texts, although these actually work counter to the apparent thinking that's generally behind this approach, which is that you should cover up any signs of mediation. But there are other things we do to texts in traditional editions that just don't fit the archive model: notably emendation. There are two problems about Renaissance texts—and plays in particular—that make emendation necessary. One is, simply, the rate of textual error. As we all know, these are texts with a fair number of misprints in them. Indeed, in two of the works by Middleton in our edition, whole blocks of text appear in the wrong order. It seems desirable that we should share our findings on such matters with readers. And the second problem, which is specific to plays, is that of sorting out and presenting to the reader information on how the work was staged. The traditional approach to this—including the remarkably interventionist step of adding extra words to the text in the form of stage directions—seems to us a very good way to go about it.

To sum up this line of argument, then: If we look at the archive as *literary* scholars rather than as scholars of printing history, it has severe problems. It suggests that the texts it presents are complete and comprehensible in themselves—when we know from our experience that we generally need to know more about them than just what happened to get printed on the page in 1620. And in its mode of presentation the archive *levels* and *dissociates* every-

---

[4] Jane Armstrong, Commissioning Editor for the Arden Shakespeare, in remarks during a panel discussion, "Editing Shakespeare," at the Literary Theory and the Practice of Editing Conference, Liverpool, July 10, 1993.

thing: it does not suggest why one text might be more interesting or pertinent than another, or how one text is related to another.

However, the approach we've taken for the Middleton edition isn't the only way to meet these needs. There are, after all, many approaches to scholarly editing. And, as I've suggested in passing, there are ways to turn the archive into something much more productive of new understanding. Elizabeth Solopova told us about one way; and David Gants's project illustrates how scholarly analysis can give us a new look at Renaissance texts from a perspective quite different from one focused on the individual author. To illustrate another way, let me talk about the other editorial project I'm currently involved in, the Women Writers Project at Brown University.

We've been operating for ten years to create documentary editions of texts in English by pre-Victorian women writers. The reason these are needed is that many people still think women didn't *do* any writing before the Victorian era, and there certainly weren't until recently many scholarly resources relating to these writers—editions and criticism are still too rare. (The superb editions that Jo Roberts created are notable exceptions.) We've tried to do something about the dearth of editions, and our texts have principally been used in classrooms. These are documentary editions, without introductions or notes, and so not ideal for all sorts of teaching, but they are at least more legible than facsimiles of the sources.

We've so far distributed texts on paper, but we've always created them in electronic form, and I'm currently leading our project to make our Renaissance texts available on the World Wide Web. The Mellon Foundation has generously funded this effort, which is called Renaissance Women Online—a name that one of my co-workers has suggested sounds like a 900-number service, although we haven't been driven that far to raise funds just yet. Within three years we'll have a hundred texts by Renaissance women writers available, and we'll keep expanding until we've done them all.

An archival emphasis is essential to what we do: we've preferred to do diplomatic editions of a lot of texts rather than critical editions of a few. And when the texts were mainly used in classrooms, there was at least a knowledgeable person in the picture, to select and help explain them. But our Web collection needs to offer more guidance, because we hope and expect that many students and scholars will be encountering it on their own, *without* the direction of a knowledgeable person. Or, to look at it another way, while we want to assist that community of knowledgeable persons, we also want to involve a lot of unknowledgeable persons and encourage their interest in women's writing.

And that's the heart of the problem we have to address in designing our Web presentation: we have to assume that most people aren't at all familiar with these writers and these texts. The person who is attracted by the general idea of looking into early women's writing but who has never read any will find a list of authors and titles rather unhelpful. If you've never heard of Ann Lok or Ester Sowernam or Eleanor Davies, you'll find it hard to choose one or another of their works to read. Access to original sources is of relatively little value if you don't know why you would want to look at those sources. Readers need help in selecting texts and authors.

The print world had a pretty good solution to this problem, which was the anthology, and there are an increasing number of good anthologies of these materials. But on the Web it's possible to guide readers to the texts they need without having to reduce the *number* or *length* of the texts, which is the unfortunate constraint that's always forced on a printed anthology.

Our approach is based on the assumption that readers may not know which texts they want to read, but they do have some idea of what research topics they're interested in. Now, with most kinds of digital libraries you can do a kind of subject searching by just searching for individual words. If you're interested in motherhood, you can look for texts that contain the word "mother." This technique is limited, though, because there are many words that may be relevant, and not all may be used; undergraduate students in particular may also not be familiar with the Renaissance vocabulary for their subject of interest. For example, searching for the word "colonialism" won't get you very far. So this text-searching approach will be available, but we are also creating something we think will be much more effective: an index to the texts that will allow readers to look at a list of topics, using modern vocabulary, and find texts that address those topics. This will be more fine-grained than library subject cataloguing, but will not attempt to be as detailed as back-of-the-book indexing generally is. And, while I've been calling it "subject indexing," it really extends beyond that category, because it will also cover genre and information about the author (such as the author's religion). We want to cover a variety of disciplinary perspectives, because we've always tried to represent the whole range of women's writing—we don't just do literary works, we also do political and philosophical texts, manuals of a practical nature, speeches, and religious tracts; and we try to keep the needs of historical as well as literary scholars in mind.

When you've selected a text by this means, it's useful to be able to find out a bit more about it; so we'll be including brief introductions and author biographies to provide such orientation. These are very much along the lines of what you get in an anthology; they aren't intended to be complete guides to the state of research and criticism. And generally, as you can see from this outline, we don't propose to do something terribly imposing to facilitate access. There are many desirable things that we're leaving out; some, like

annotation, we hope to do later; others are being addressed by other projects—for example, the Orlando project at the University of Alberta is developing an electronic history of women's literature. But the access features that
we are offering are the crucial ones for our project, we think: they'll serve to
get people started on reading particular texts that are relevant to their interests,
and once they've gotten that far they'll be ready to draw on other resources to
go farther. Our great hope is that in a few years Renaissance studies will be
divided into two groups of people: those who are happily using our collection
to advance their work, and those who can't figure out why everyone seems to
be always talking about these writers they never heard of like Anne Askew
and Johanna Cartwright.

So our approach in this endeavor, while very different from that of the
Middleton edition, is nevertheless directed towards one of the same goals, that
of facilitating understanding of the works in question. To state my view one
final time: archives are a great thing, but the initially appealing idea of
refraining from all apparent mediation and organization of the materials only
leaves readers to impose their own organization, when a different organization
and conceptualization may be appropriate: for instance, one in which creating
literary history involves looking at a wide range of writers, rather than just the
ones you know about already. Editions have always been powerful tools for
shaping the way we see authors and texts, and we have to direct that same
power as it inheres in electronic editions, rather than pretending it's not there.

Index

Note: The Index is alphabetized word-for-word; initial *A, An,* and *The* are ignored. Footnotes that document entries in the text are cited in the form: 149–150+n1; footnotes that are complete in themselves are cited in the form: 19.n24.

Renaissance English Text Society

M. T. Jones-Davies, University of Paris-Sorbonne
David Norbrook, Magdalen College, Oxford
Sergio Rossi, University of Milan
Germaine Warkentin, Victoria University in the University of Toronto

The Renaissance English Text Society was established to publish literary texts, chiefly nondramatic, of the period 1475–1660. Dues are $25.00 per annum ($15.00, graduate students; life membership is available at $500.00). Members receive the text published for each year of membership. The Society sponsors panels at such annual meetings as those of the Modern Language Association, the Renaissance Society of America, and the Medieval Congress at Kalamazoo. General inquiries should be addressed to the president, Arthur Kinney, Department of English, University of Massachusetts, Amherst, Mass. 01002, USA. New members should apply to M. Di Cesare, Department of Literature and Language, University of North Carolina, Asheville, NC 28804.

Copies of volumes X–XII may be purchased from Associated University Presses, 440 Forsgate Drive, Cranbury, NJ 08512. Members may order copies of earlier volumes still in print or of later volumes from XIII, at special member prices, from the Treasurer.

FIRST SERIES

VOL. I. *Merie Tales of the Mad Men of Gotam* by A. B., edited by Stanley J. Kahrl, and *The History of Tom Thumbe,* by R. I., edited by Curt F. Buhler, 1965. (o.p.)

VOL. II. Thomas Watson's Latin *Amyntas,* edited by Walter F. Staton, Jr., and Abraham Fraunce's translation *The Lamentations of Amyntas,* edited by Franklin M. Dickey, 1967.

SECOND SERIES

VOL. III. *The dyaloge called Funus,* A Translation of Erasmus's Colloquy (1534), and *A very pleasaunt & fruitful Diologe called The Epicure,* Gerrard's Translation of Erasmus's Colloquy (1545), edited by Robert R. Allen, 1969.

VOL. IV. *Leicester's Ghost* by Thomas Rogers, edited by Franklin B. Williams, Jr., 1972.

THIRD SERIES

VOLS. V–VI. *A Collection of Emblemes, Ancient and Moderne,* by George Wither, with an introduction by Rosemary Freeman and bibliographical notes by Charles S. Hensley, 1975. (o.p.)

ᚹRTS

ᚹEᚱIEVAᛚ & RENAISSANCE TEXTS & STUᚱIES
is the major publishing program of the
Arizona Center for Medieval and Renaissance Studies
at Arizona State University, Tempe, Arizona.

ᚹRTS emphasizes books that are needed —
texts, translations, and major research tools.

ᚹRTS aims to publish the highest quality scholarship
in attractive and durable format at modest cost.